W9-AFV-756

Judgments,
Choices,
and Decisions

THE WILEY MANAGEMENT SERIES ON PROBLEM SOLVING, DECISION MAKING, AND STRATEGIC THINKING

David W. Ewing, Series Editor

JUDGMENTS, CHOICES, AND DECISIONS

Effective Management through Self-Knowledge

Warren J. Keegan

JOHN WILEY & SONS

New York • Chichester • Brisbane • Toronto • Singapore

This publication is designed to provide accurate and
authoritative information in regard to the subject
matter covered. It is sold with the understanding that
the publisher is not engaged in rendering legal, accounting,
or other professional service. If legal advice or other
expert assistance is required, the services of a competent
professional person should be sought. *From a Declaration
of Principles jointly adopted by a Committee of the
American Bar Association and a Committee of Publishers.*

Library of Congress Cataloging in Publication Data:

Keegan, Warren J.

Judgments, choices, and decisions.

(The Wiley management series on problem solving,
decision making, and strategic thinking)

Includes bibliographies and index.

1. Management—Psychological aspects. 2. Typology
(Psychology) I. Title. II. Series.

HD58.7.K42   1984   658.4'094   83-19786

ISBN 0-471-86834-5

Printed in the United States of America

10 9 8 7 6 5 4 3 2 1

Preface

My purpose in writing this book is to help managers and would-be managers become better performers and competitors. Most managers have the necessary functional skills (in marketing and finance, for example) to succeed. Where many fall down is in failing to understand why they behave and make decisions the way they do. Like most people, managers view the world in ways which reflect both their own background and the culture of their organizations. They live and work with a point of view which they believe is realistic.The opposite, however, may be the case.

Although the Edsel story is used so frequently, the question of how the most extensive and expensive market research campaign in the history of American business could be such a miserable failure is still crucial. One reason, which I bring up and which constitutes a major theme of this book, is that most of the decision makers at Ford were "birds of a feather flocking together." That is, they were similar types who never questioned assumptions or decisions—until the roof fell in. In fact, the case can be made that the auto industry, for example, kept right on going in the same way through a series of collapsed roofs.

But people are people and difficult to change. So, my goal is not to change my readers, but help them come to a reasonable level of self-understanding. If they can understand how they view the world and the impact this view has on their decision style, then the decisions will be better and more thoughtful.

Where I do try to influence readers to change is by expanding their ability to respond on different levels and in different ways to problems and opportunities. Most managers pride themselves on an ability to analyze a situation and think their way through to a solution. Fine! But there will be times when analysis and thought may not be the way to go. You may research an idea or proposal until the competition snaps it up or the market passes it by. In some cases intuition is the most appropriate response. My point is not to downplay analysis and thinking—if that is your style—but to recognize that a strength in one situation may not be appropriate in another. And if I have one major piece of advice, it is to avoid staffing a company with all of one type. If you do, I hope you enjoy the proverbial ride to hell on a roller coaster.

Many people contributed to the development of this book. My students at The George Washington University and General Electric's Management Development Institute explored the applications of the theory to management in classroom, seminar, and report discussions. Colleagues and clients were of great assistance in commenting on my work and in sharing their own perceptions and insights. Ken Michel, formerly at GE and now with GTE, was instrumental in research at GE which clearly established the relationship between type and task performance. Robert Allio, Katherine Evans,

David Heenan, Chikara Higashi, Jim Stoner, and Peter Vaill made very helpful comments at many stages in the development of my research and writing. Dr. Joseph B. Wheelwright and Isabel Briggs Myers were most helpful in sharing their observations and insights. Thayer Greene and Nathan Schwartz-Salant helped me explore my own type and the dynamics of Jung's psychology.

John Mahaney, my editor at Wiley, saw the need and the potential for this book and has been an unfailing source of support, encouragement, and critical insight during its development.

I owe a special debt to a special colleague, Professor Jerry Harvey of the School of Government and Business Administration, The George Washington University. Jerry has read every word of this manuscript from the earliest GWU working paper to the present book. His enthusiasm for this project and his conviction that it should and could be done have kept me going at times when I felt that the wisest course would be to abandon ship. Jerry is the prototype of the introverted intuitive: an original thinker with the courage to express new, and often unpopular, ideas. I am grateful for his many ideas and comments, our innumerable discussions, his friendship and support, and most of all for his magnificent sense of humor.

As a professor at The George Washington University, New York University, and Pace University during the preparation of this manuscript, I have been fortunate in having supportive and encouraging deans and department chairpersons. At GWU, Dean Norma Loeser and Ben Burdetsky, my department chairperson, were generous in giving time and other assistance to support my research. Henry Assail at New York University was helpful in arranging a visiting professorship, and Tony Bonaparte, my dean at Pace University, has been supportive and helpful in providing the resources to bring this project to completion.

All of my personal friends and family have been subjected to my fascination with type: I would especially like to mention Isabel Wellisz, Dr. Alfred D. Sunderwirth, Alison Ruml, Marian Fuller, and Cathy Allen.

If you would like to share any of your experiences or insights about type and how it has helped you to perform more effectively as a manager or professional, I would love to hear from you. Just drop a note to me in care of John Wiley & Sons, 605 Third Avenue, New York, NY 10158.

Of course, it goes without saying that I am solely responsible for any errors or flaws in this book.

WARREN J. KEEGAN

Rye, New York
December 1983

Contents

Judgments,
Choices,
and Decisions

Introduction

Because management is the "art of the possible," managers need to understand themselves and the workers who are charged with carrying out plans. Seemingly, there is a lot of assistance available; indeed, the make-up of the successful manager is the focus today of a vast educational, consulting, and publishing establishment.

Yet, despite the attention given to it, the ideal manager remains shrouded in myth and mystery; yesterday's hero is often today's villain. Managers are an enigmatic lot, and it is difficult to identify the good ones until a sufficient track record has been established—a record that can sometimes be upset overnight by seemingly inexplicable mistakes. Business case studies abound with examples of the charismatic leader who falls on his or her face as manager, the brilliant detail person who fails to grasp the big picture, the super salesperson who can get the business but cannot run the company.

Today it is fashionable to blame business schools for

Adapted with permission from Warren J. Keegan, "Managing the Personality Puzzle," *Planning Review*, March 1982, pp. 12–15.

turning out people who are obsessed with the bottom line and short-term goals, for creating managers who can theorize brilliantly but cannot deal with day-to-day realities. The professors, in turn, say this is not the fault of the schools, which are only providing what business says it needs, but of business itself. Business, they say, enforces short-term values and, by no longer bringing people up through the ranks, deprives them of hands-on experience that in the past gave not only a thorough understanding of the company but created a sense of loyalty missing in M.B.A. careerists.

The beliefs that guide today's executives—and today's corporations—have shaped the American business character by focusing on certain discrete characteristics of people. In the Western world, value is placed exclusively on thinking, and the thinking type has prevailed. Consequently, many American organizations are seriously unbalanced in the values that guide them at the top and throughout the various levels of the management hierarchy.

According to research by Professors Skinner and Sasser of the Harvard Business School, effective managers, defined as managers with the greatest positive impact on their organizations, are versatile and inconsistent.[1] They found that effective managers constantly varied their methods, priorities, and ways of dealing with superiors and subordinates. These findings fly straight in the face of the assumption that there is an ideal management style. Although this is surprising at first, when one thinks about it, these conclusions make sense. Managers are needed to deal with the unknown.

---

[1]Wickham Skinner and W. Earl Sasser, "Effective Managers are Versatile and Inconsistent," in Management Analysis Center, Inc., *Implementing Strategy* (Cambridge, Mass.).

If jobs were perfectly predictable, companies could be set on "automatic pilot" and run according to a formula.

Effective managers express Emerson's maxim in their work: "Inconsistency is the mark of genius." The less effective managers in the Skinner-Sasser study were much more predictable. Although there is an infinite number of ways to fail, each of the low-performing managers failed in the same manner from one situation to the next.

Sixty years ago, psychiatrist Carl Gustav Jung developed what is one of many examples of man's efforts to *type* the vast diversity of human beings. And, because of its accuracy in identifying characteristics and predicting behaviors, Jung's typology is again receiving attention, but this time the renewed interest is from professionals involved in the education of managers. Those in business who use Jung's typology as an educational tool believe it offers a true insight into why people succeed or fail, and how they do it.

Jung's theory features two dimensions, the first of which is attitude. The attitudes are *introversion* and *extroversion*. The theory says introverts respond slowly to situations, or the demands of others, as they require time to integrate and assimilate outside information. Extroverts, on the other hand, tend to respond quickly and are oriented toward action rather than reflection and introspection. To be sure, extroverts can be described as experiencing aloneness as a burden, as opposed to introverts who are often refreshed by periods of solitude.

In addition to attitude, Jung said people are inclined to lead with one of four functions in the way they customarily solve problems. He identified these functions as: (1) intuition, (2) thinking, (3) feeling, and (4) sensing (Figure 1).

Figure 1. Jung's four functions: intuition, thinking, feeling, and sensing.

Intuitives concentrate on possibilities; they are holistic in handling problems and impatient with details. They often "intuit" solutions and fail to back them up with data, having gone on to something else.

Thinkers are analytical, precise, and logical, and tend to process information from beginning to end. They intellectualize, often ignoring the emotional or feeling aspects of a situation. Thus they often appear to be ruthless or uncaring; not so, they are just thinking.

Feelers are interested in the feelings of others, dislike intellectual analysis, and follow their own likes and dislikes. They enjoy working with people and are capable of great loyalty.

Sensers see things as they are and have great respect for facts. They have an enormous capacity for detail, seldom make errors, and are good at close, demanding tasks.

The best way to show how attitudes and functions combine to produce a *type* is through example. For instance, Albert Einstein can accurately be labeled an introverted thinker. Supremely happy in the contemplation of ideas, Einstein simply was not connected to the conventional scientific theories of his day. As a youth he was a poor student, unable to relate to the current teaching of his instructors. Einstein's theory thus came out of his own creativity.

Dwight D. Eisenhower, whose success as a general and President stemmed from his ability to reflect the collective values and feelings of his time, can best be described as an extroverted feeler. Charles de Gaulle, on the other hand, was a successful introverted intuitive, whose effectiveness was based on a subjective vision. During World War II and the Algerian crisis, de Gaulle was inspired by a dream of France's greatness. He ignored the majority view and held to this inner vision. Thus, each of these men was true to his own nature and effective in different ways.

It is interesting to note that Western culture generally overvalues the thinker and undervalues intuitives, sensers, and feelers. Only one-fourth of good planning involves the use of skill and technique. The other three-quarters include monitoring daily performance, getting commitment, and freeing management's imagination and creativity.

One problem that often arises in planning occurs when a financially ailing company, under stress and freezing up, recognizes only one alternative or solution. The importance of planning as a tool used to assist a company in making the right choices to ensure top performance cannot be underestimated. Too much management technique overemphasizes thinking, while individual values, commitment, and motivation are often ignored.

In businesses where executives have "flocked" together according to typology, there is a tunnel vision that can seriously warp a company's perspective and performance. For instance, the founder and president of a company specializing in a complex packaging technique is an introverted intuitive. Recognizing the technique's advantages, he creatively exploited them and, in doing so, established his company as a leader in the industry. But as the industry matured, the critical success requirements shifted from creative product development to cost management.

The president, however, retained his one-sided interest in creativity and the development of new ideas. What did he do? He brought in an M.B.A. who could be described as a "bird of a feather," the same person typologically, and the two of them continued to generate new ideas and blue-sky opportunities. What was needed was a person who could come into the business and manage costs and turn the company into a low-cost, high-volume competitor. Instead, the company diversified into new and exciting areas, rather than concentrating on the job of managing costs, and the business soon declined in profitability and lost its competitive edge.

A FEELING STYLE:
THE JAPANESE BUSINESSPERSON

Japanese business and culture are interesting because they emphasize feeling values. It is not that they ignore the other functions, but the emphasis on feeling is the key to expressing the other functions. Indeed, Japanese senior executives draw on subordinates unusually well, and in dealings with outsiders, they do all the talking while junior executives listen and agree. This sounds disastrous; one person apparently doing all the thinking. But in a Japanese firm, everybody is free to speak openly, to pursue their own ideas, and to be respected and valued—the so-called *Ringi* system.

One does not need to dwell on the success of the Japanese. One way of looking at it is to take all the industries where the society has focused its resources, and see what is happening in world-scale competition. So far, in each industry—cameras, automobiles, televisions, and motorcycles—to mention only a few, there has been an expression of leadership and impressive success. This success underscores the value and importance of feeling that the Japanese place in business. They call it "sincerity"—another term for feeling.

International Business Machines Corp. exemplifies

this feeling philosophy in American business. The corporate giant has been described as a firm that "smothers its employees with a dazzling array of womb-to-tomb benefits, ingenious motivational perks and sophisticated self-improvement programs."[2] As a result, IBM is universally regarded by corporate recruiting firms as the "best company to work for" in the United States among major corporations.

Under the direction of Thomas Watson, Sr., one aspect that was unmistakenly distinctive about IBM was Watson's idea that it was a family. A family is something that people are not expelled from for incompetence. A family is where people are connected.

The famous "Think" slogan that Watson wallpapered IBM with was his way of accessing the thinking function. Watson was a feeler, and he needed a constant reminder of the importance of thinking. Watson, for example, did not see the possibilities in computers. But the feeling atmosphere at IBM allowed a lot of the original work to be done underground. The organization was large enough and creative enough to permit good, solid thinking, and this flexibility has undoubtedly contributed to IBM's *esprit de corps*.

SENSING

Another function consistently devalued in favor of thinking is sensing, the acute awareness of the object. John Ware Lincoln, an architect, who retired in 1970 as chairman of the design division at the Rhode Island School of Design, deplores the lack of this function in design students.

---

[2]Allan J. Mayer and Michael Ruby, "One Firm's Family," *Newsweek*, Nov. 21, 1977, pp. 82–87.

In trying to teach students how to run machines and make models of the products they were attempting to design, he found that many of them could not draw three-dimensional concepts, could not cut a piece of wood square, or sharpen a knife or chisel. "They had been too busy," he says, "in elementary and high schools with 'intellectual' pursuits." The faculty's consensus was that the students were too old by this time to develop hand-eye coordination. "We learned, after four years of desultory craftsmanship, that we were not Swiss and that, if we want to return the country to its former supremacy in science, mechanical skills, and the arts, elementary schools must continue the valuable manual exercises begun in kindergarten."[3] Thus, if schools focus exclusively on intellectual development, the sensate skills suffer.

A FULL EXPRESSION OF LIFE

Businessmen, educators, and other professionals must recognize the inherent value of developing both attitudes and functions. Jung did not favor one function or one attitude over another, as they all have their place in his theory, but the individual that has mastered each function and both attitudes will surely experience life to the fullest.

Life and business demand the exercise of both perception and judgment. In other words, function and attitude are equally valuable; yet as individuals we are quite different in the way our minds function. The organization that recognizes this basic truth and expresses it by respecting and integrating individual talents assures itself of a vast pool of human potential.

[3]John Ware Lincoln, "The American Handicap in Developing Superior Craftsmen," *The New York Times*, Feb. 13, 1981, p. A26.

This book is about psychological types, and how knowledge of types can expand your self-knowledge and your ability to be more effective as a manager and as a person. One of the ways that type knowledge can help you be more effective is to expand your ability to respond on different levels and in different ways to problems and opportunities. In effect, you can teach yourself through knowledge of type to be more versatile and inconsistent.

Jung believed that if people understood their differences and achieved balance in themselves and their organizations, both individuals and groups would be healthier and more successful. This book is an application of his theory and insight to the tasks and responsibilities of the manager. It is said that it takes at least 50 years for a major new idea to take root in the social sciences. *Psychological Types* was first published in 1921, so it is now 62 years since the concept of psychological types was introduced to the world. Jung's theory has stood the test of time in the fields of psychology and psychiatry. It has become established as a profound insight into how the mind functions. I believe that the time has come to take this insight beyond the world of the psychologist and psychiatrist and into that of the practicing manager. The purpose of this book is to make this theory accessible to the wider audience of managers and professionals who could benefit from its insight into how our minds actually work.

In reviewing the plethora of planning and decision-making models that are currently available, one realizes that while each has value, each is incomplete. The typology theory of Jung is almost complete in the sense that it touches on both functions of perception and both functions of judgment and their relationship to each other. Nothing is left out: there are no functions of perception or judgment that could be added, and none could be taken away. What is omitted from the theory is the relationship of memory and beliefs to the functions, and I have focused on that in this book. Therefore, this is a complete theory.

1

The Personality Puzzle: What's Your Decision Style?

By the time we discovered we were introverts, it was too late to do anything about it.

BOB ELLIOTT of BOB and RAY

One of the first tasks of management is "know thyself." Self-knowledge is the beginning of managerial wisdom, because it provides a foundation for the clear perception of others, which, along with the perception of self, is essential if there is to be any kind of realism and reality in planning and action. As you will discover in Chapter 2, most people, including business executives, live and work with what they believe is a realistic point of view and orientation. The opposite may be the case. Many people and organizations feel comfortable with a point of view and perception of reality that no longer hold true.

In some cases, the roof may be about to cave in and no one knows it. Take, for example, the case of the Coors company. Since its founding in 1873, Coors has always been noted for two things: its "brewed with pure Rocky Mountain Spring Water" slogan, and its obsession with quality and control. Coors was a family company, with a single product, Coors, serving a regional market from a single brewery. William Coors and his brother, Joe, shared the management of the company. Both were noted for extreme conservatism. By sheer chance, Coors became a mystique beer. Because it was not available nationally, because it had a reputation for quality, and because it just happened to be a light beer in a market that was moving toward lighter beers, Coors found itself in the delightful position of brewing a product that literally sold itself. Demand exceeded supply, and the product was placed on allocation.

Since the product sold itself, Coors largely ignored marketing and concentrated on brewing. The company's first real difficulties came with the introduction of Miller Lite in 1975. Lite's success blocked Coors's growth. In opening up a new segment, it cannibalized the Coors's franchise. Then came a strike in 1977, and an AFL-CIO product boycott that was triggered by the conservative politics of the Coors brothers. The strike and the boycott resulted in a sales decline through 1978. In addition, aggressive competition from Miller Lite and Anheuser-Bush began to make inroads into Coors's markets.

The shock of this decline led to a decision to introduce Coors Light in 1978, in spite of the fact that Bill Coors had said that Coors would never sell any beer other than the basic Coors brand. It also led to a decision to advertise the product that had, up until that point, literally sold itself.

TYPOLOGICAL ANALYSIS

William and Joseph Coors had an introverted management style. They did things their way, and until the disastrous 1977 experience, they believed that it worked. There was little extroversion, or sensitivity to the outer world, and there was little empathy for people. Indeed, this style had put the company in the number four position in brewing in the national market. Coors was famous because it had *not* been marketed. President Ford and Secretary Kissinger imported it to Washington. Famous actors like Paul Newman and Clint Eastwood swore by it. It was the "in" beer.

The impact of Miller and the strike did not result in a speedy response. In true introverted fashion, the Coors brothers stuck to their course. They resisted and rejected information that indicated their strategy was not working. In doing this, they followed the tradition of a long line of managers who refused to see the reality of a changing situation, especially a painful and difficult change. Coors began to turn around only when they responded to what was happening in the marketplace. This response was coming out of their extroverted attitude. It was there; all they needed to do was to acknowledge it and let it enable them to "read" the situation. Once they had opened up to a perception of the situation, they could then act on their judgment.

The terms *extroversion* and *introversion* were first used by C. G. Jung, the Swiss psychoanalyst, in his book *Psychological Types*.[1] The theoretical foundation

---

[1] C. G. Jung, *Psychological Types*. In The Collected Works of C. G. Jung, Vol. 6, Bollingen Series 20. (Princeton, N.J., Princeton University Press, 1976). (Originally published in German as *Psychologische Typen*, Zurich: Rascher Verlag, 1921.)

of this book is based on Jung's original work. The basic theory of type is that people approach life with different *attitudes* toward the outer and inner world, and with different preferences for ways of perceiving and judging reality, known as *functions.*

Many people expect to discover good and bad psychological types and are either delighted or disappointed, depending upon their point of view, when they discover that there are no good or bad types. Type is a part of nature, and there is no "good" or "bad" in nature. The attitude of people toward type however, is typically framed in a good or bad mold. One of the new dimensions of knowledge that you should get from this book is an appreciation of the value of each of the different types.

EXTROVERSION AND INTROVERSION

The pleasure of knowing that differences are based on type was shared recently in one of my executive MBA classes at Pace University. The group was particularly lively and expressive, and had developed a strong *esprit de corps.* Much of the exuberance of the group was generated in the back row of the class by three participants who sat in the right rear seats of the class and expressed themselves quite strongly and frequently. I gave this class my own *Keegan Type Indicator,* a self-scoring instrument, which measures preferences for attitude and function. The results confirmed what everyone knew: the three participants in the back row were raving extroverts. This knowledge was of particular comfort to one of the students in the class, an introvert who was in a study group with these three. At last he knew why he felt so uncomfortable in the study group: he was the odd man out. The knowledge that there were type differences made it OK for the introvert to be an introvert. Without this knowledge, there was probably at least a small part of him that felt out of place and that wanted to be more like the others, or that would become critical of the others. The same danger existed for the extroverts in the group. Since they were in the majority, they probably were not likely to wish that they were introverts, but there was a danger that they would feel critical of their introverted group member because he was not like them. Indeed, for management, the most significant and important implication of type is the insight it provides into complementarity and its power in forming management teams or task forces.

REALITY: ATTITUDE AND FUNCTION

Every manager is ultimately concerned with the task of perceiving and dealing with reality. These tasks are approached in different ways by different people. There are three dimensions of the psyche by which we are oriented at work (and at play):

Attitude.   Either introverted (inner directed) or extroverted (outer directed).

Perception.   Either sensation perception, via the five senses, or intuitive perception, via the sixth sense.

Judgment.   Choice or conclusions arrived at through thinking (logical processes) or feeling (personal values).

The attitudes and functions are opposed in the sense that one does not use them simultaneously. (See Figure 1.1.) This means that if you are thinking, you are not simultaneously feeling and vice versa. If you are perceiving via sensation, you are not simultaneously perceiving

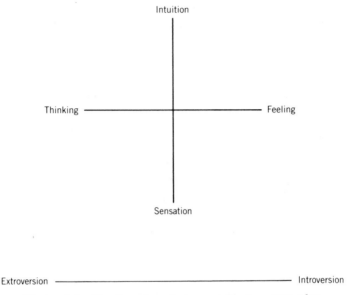

Figure 1.1. The four functions and the two attitudes.

via intuition. Each person has a preference for one of the four functions, which is known as his or her superior function. The opposite of the superior function, or a person's strength, is the inferior function, or the person's greatest weakness. For example, if your superior function is thinking, your weakest or inferior function will be feeling. If your superior function is sensation, your inferior or weakest function will be intuition.

Similarly, if you are an extrovert, your typical way of relating to work and life will be via your extroversion. If you are an introvert, your typical way of relating will be via your introversion. One manager will be outer directed, the other inner directed.

At first glance, it might appear that extroversion is a superior attitude for business and management. There is no question of the need for a strong sense of objective reality in management. Every manager must have the ability to function as an extrovert. However, there is also no question of the need for inner direction and orientation in management. The manager who is too extroverted will not be able to stick to a course of action because he or she will be too sensitive to the outer world. Every manager needs to be in touch with his or her introverted as well as extroverted side.

It is important to recognize that type refers to behavior, not to personality. Instead of saying "so-and-so is a thinker," which is "typing" the person, it is more accurate to say this behavior expresses thinking. People are so complex that, while the temptation may be great to type someone as one of sixteen types, this is worse than not typing the person at all. Moreover, it is extremely difficult to type anyone on the basis of observed behavior. Indeed, Jung himself is reported to have said that you will never know a person's real type until 50 years after that person's death. He also said, "My typology is not meant to stick labels on people at first sight."

Dr. James Hillman has emphasized that typology has no "hard edges"—one is not either this or that; one is more or less one thing or the other. Hard-edge distinctions are represented by a "class," not a "typology." "Extroversion does not *per se* exclude introversion,"[2] he says. But we begin to use types as classes, and we begin to classify ourselves and others as types, "either this or that." Hillman points out that almost 18,000 "trait names" exist in English that are used to describe human personality. These include ethnic epithets that are no longer used, nationalistic and stereotypical descriptions, and new psychological jargon. The theory should be

[2]James Hillman, "Types, Images and Perceptions of Uniqueness," lecture, C. G. Jung Foundation, 1977.

applied not to "typing" people but to understanding behavior. It is an invaluable guide to understanding how decisions can be arrived at and why people sometimes do the things they do.

It is useful to know that not all people function in the same way and that the other person's contribution can be as valuable as our own, but in a different way. With an understanding of type and where the other person is coming from, the quality of decision-making and the ability of people to respect each other and get along will be enhanced because people will be acting from their own strengths and respect the strengths of others. At the same time, knowledge of one's own strengths—and weaknesses—enables us to more effectively use our talent and to relate constructively and noncompetitively to the strengths and weaknesses of others.

HOW PSYCHIC ENERGY FLOWS

The direction of energy flow and the locus of orientation in life are illustrated in Figure 1.2 (see page 24). At the core of the psyche is the unconscious, or that which we are unaware of—that which is hidden. This base reservoir of the field of the psyche contains the collective unconscious, which Jung calls the individual's racial memory. One of Jung's most fascinating discoveries (which was based on his observation that the dreams of primitive tribesmen of Uganda and modern Europeans were, in part, identical) was that this racial memory, or collective unconscious, contains elements that are universal: the Masai tribesman and the European intellectual share, at this level, a common racial heritage.

The next layer of the psyche is the personal unconscious or the memory and belief system which orients us. Think of experience as rain that flows into the sea of memory. Some is lost or evaporates on its way, and some is distorted by pollutants. This is especially true of early childhood experience. The important distinction is between the personal and collective unconscious. The personal is based on our own life experience. The collective is a racial memory. To illustrate: everyone has the experience of a personal father and mother, or a substitute for father or mother. This experience is the basis for the personal unconscious. Everyone also has a memory of the archetypal great mother and father, which is not personal but collective. Much confusion can develop in the unconscious when the personal and collective contents are not differentiated. The archetypal great mother, for example, is a source of life and nourishment that vastly exceeds the capacity and ability of a personal mother to sustain and nourish. The personal mother is a person, not an archetype.

The next layer is the sense of conscious identity that we sometimes call the personality. Part of this is the persona or mask we present to the world, or the part we play in life. This might be the mask of the artist, the taxi driver, the lawyer, the doctor, the professor, the minister, the banker, or the executive. This persona or mask is absolutely necessary to function in the world, but individuals differ in the extent to which they identify with the persona. Some personae are quite powerful because they attract very strong projections from most people. The minister, for example, is a person who carries the persona of the spiritual and the holy. The person who is a minister may be an ordinary person with or without a calling to the vocation. Whatever the case, the projection of what people idealize in a "minister" may confuse the men and women who play the part and make it difficult for them to express their one "shadow," or that side of their nature of which they are unaware.

Another aspect of personality is the sense of who we

are. Some people feel, and are, happy and empowered. Others feel, and are, impotent and depressed. Most of us fall between this pillar and post. As we get older, the shape of personality under ideal conditions becomes more and more real in the sense that it expresses what we really are, as opposed to what we would like to be, or our worst fears of what we might be.

Of course, each of the "fields" interacts with the other. Our memory and beliefs have a profound effect on our personality. If we can change our beliefs, we will change our personality. Some people believe that it is wrong to be angry. As a result, they repress their anger instead of expressing it in life. If we can convince such persons that it is OK to be angry, that being angry is just part of being, it often has a striking effect on their personality and experience of life. Some people are oriented by memories that dominate their lives. Often, these powerful memories are associated with an early trauma, such as sexual molestation in childhood, or they may be associated with a recent trauma, such as a mugging. Whatever the event, a memory can begin to dominate a person's life.

The personality then is really the sum of the sense of identity and the system of conscious and unconscious memory, beliefs, and emotion. People vary in the ways in which they are related to their unconscious. The truly creative individual, whether an artist, scientist, or business person, has a positive relation to the wellsprings of creative energy in the unconscious. Most fiction writers say, for example, that they know that they are really writing their story or novel when it begins to write itself. Often, characters turn out quite differently than the author had expected because, in the process of writing, the character takes on a life of its own. This is an example of creatively drawing on the unconscious. Creative executives invent and come up with new solutions by tapping the wellsprings of their unconscious creative energy. Every major breakthrough in art, business, and science is a creative act that taps the unconscious.

ATTITUDE: EXTROVERSION AND INTROVERSION

Extroversion and introversion are terms which describe the direction of energy flow in the individual and the primary mode of orientation. As shown in Figure 1.2, the extrovert is oriented by the outer world of objects and things, while the introvert is oriented by the inner world of beliefs, memory and thought. For the extrovert, the energy flows from the outside world to the inner world, while for the introvert, the energy flows from the inner world to the outside. In both attitudes, the inner and outer worlds connect, but the process is reversed.

The extrovert is characterized by a positive relation to objects (people and things), while the introvert is characterized by an abstracting one. In adjusting or adapting to life, extroverted people orient themselves predominantly by outward, collective norms; the spirit of the times; the perceived values, feelings, and expectations of others. The introverted person is more comfortable dealing with the inner psychic world as opposed to the outer world of people and things. For the extrovert, being alone is often experienced as a burden, whereas for the introvert, it is often a relief. Jung's extrovert corresponds to David Riesman's "outer-directed" man; the introvert to Riesman's "inner-directed" man.

Of course, everyone expresses both extroversion and introversion in their lives. Nevertheless, most people tend to be predominantly extroverted or introverted. There are strong cultural attitudes toward these orien-

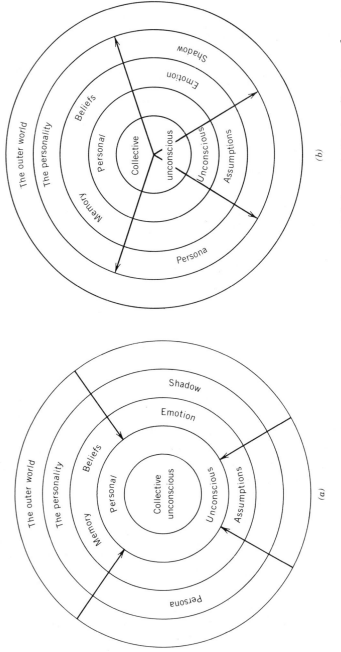

Figure 1.2. (a) Extroversion: Energy flows from the outer to the inner world. Arrow indicates direction of energy flow. (b) Introversion: Energy flows from the inner to the outer world. Arrow indicates direction of energy flow.

24

tations. In the U.S. business culture, introversion is often regarded with suspicion. There is a stereotyped image of the introvert as a shy, retiring, passive person, as opposed to the open, easy-going, action-oriented extrovert. These popular misconceptions confuse personality and attitude. Attitude (extroversion–introversion) refers to the orientation—whether one is oriented by the inner or the outer world. Personality traits or qualities such as leadership have nothing to do with introversion/extroversion. It is useful to identify your own attitude and to separate attitude from personality. Perhaps you feel that you have achieved the correct balance between these two opposed orientations, or you may conclude that you need to get more in touch with your inner direction (your introverted side) or with the objective world (your extroverted side).

PERCEPTION: SENSATION AND INTUITION

Perception is "the act or faculty of apprehending by means of the senses or of the mind,"[3] that is, becoming aware of something. The two functions of perception are sensation and intuition. Sensation is perception by means of the five senses: sight, hearing, taste, touch, and smell. Sensation is the function of the mind or psyche that tells us that something exists. Sensation perceives by attentiveness to sensory stimuli. It focuses on the parts and seeks to move from the parts to the whole. Someone who has a preference for perceiving with this function is known as a sensation type. Sensation types are observers. They notice the details of life. I

[3]*The Random House College Dictionary* (New York: Random House, 1978).

once saw the president of a company insist that a company memo be restapled because the staples were not in perfect horizontal alignment. This is an example of a sensate's attention to detail.

Another function of perception, as opposed to sensation, is intuition. Intuition is perception via what is sometimes called the "sixth sense." Intuition apprehends the totality of a situation—it is holistic perception. Whereas sensation tells us that something exists, intuition tells us about the possibilities in the "something." This might be a person or a situation. Many people use the term "gut feeling" or "hunch" to describe their intuitive function. Intuition is often found in finance. For example, Ira Kuhlik, a gold trader, has been extraordinarily successful in predicting the market. When asked about his methods, Kuhlik credits "intuition." But he buttresses his intuition with thinking and sensation; he has read every book published on commodities trading; he takes voice lessons so that he can shout all day without getting laryngitis; he wears red shorts for luck; and he takes vitamins. Research, however, doesn't help. "Very often the market ignores fundamentals," he says.[4] Intuitive types have an expectant orientation toward life.

All of us perceive the world with both these functions, with either predominating at different times, but everyone has an innate preference for one or the other. The sensation type, who typically takes in information via the five senses, is most comfortable when attending to the details and specifics of a situation. This individual breaks down every situation into isolated bits of information and feels most comfortable when he or she has gathered the "hard facts" that describe the situation.

[4]*The Wall Street Journal,* October 1, 1979, p. 1.

Sensation types make good engineers, draftspersons, and designers because they are ruthless in chasing down details. Highly intuitive people, on the other hand, often have a weak grasp on the real world: The prototypical "absent-minded professor" is someone who is high on intuition and low on sensation.

A basic tenet of the type model is that these functions, sensation and intuition, are equally valid ways of perceiving. It is important to emphasize this proposition because many individuals often fall into the trap of valuing one function at the expense of another. The sensation "type," for example, will ask for "the facts" and act as if the only valid facts are those which can be perceived via the five senses. These people look askance at intuitives, whose sometimes brilliant solutions cannot be backed up by "the facts." Both types may or may not be right, and the solutions they will each find will probably be opposed. Intuitives—unless they are in charge of the project—will be at a disadvantage in not being able to "prove" their solutions. If, however, intuitives are operating as a group, sometimes they can "tap" into each other's perception and achieve a great deal of understanding with a minimum of words. This leaves the sensation type at a complete loss.

Unfortunately, sensation drives out intuition in organizations. In strategic business-unit planning, there is a mechanism that forces conservatism into the consideration of future events and so tends to squeeze out intuitive judgments if they cannot be thoroughly documented.

The onus attached to the "intuitive" function in hierarchical institutions is based on the cultural bias in favor of the factual and the concrete. The exception to this is the advertising agency that recognizes the critical importance and fragile nature of the creative idea.

This understanding is the basis for the tender care, respect, and even awe of the creative in advertising. This, however, is unusual. The typical organization is dominated by thinker and sensate styles, and these types are naturally suspicious of intuitive ideas.

JUDGMENT: THINKING AND FEELING

The two functions of judgment are thinking and feeling. Thinking is the function that seeks to generalize, to find cause and effect, to sort out objective, logical conclusions. Thinking types have an analytical attitude. Feeling, an equally valid but opposed function of judgment, seeks to individualize or particularize. Feeling is the function that expresses personal valuation. Feeling takes into account whatever is subjectively important to the individual and then makes a decision on the basis of personal values. Feeling types personalize. Thinking is the function that tells us what something is; feeling is the function that tells us whether or not we like it.

Everyone of course uses both functions to make decisions. Significantly, however, everyone has a preference for either thinking or feeling in making judgments. In our culture, thinking is a highly regarded and well-understood function. Our entire educational system is focused on developing and differentiating the thinking function, and our culture worships at the altar of thinking.

Feeling, the opposed function of judgment, is, in contrast, often misunderstood and undervalued. The chief executive officer is not supposed to say, "I feel." He or she is supposed to say, "I know," asserts David Mahoney, Chairman of Norton Simon. "So we deify the word instinct by calling it judgment. But any attempt to deny instinct is to deny identity. It's the most current thing. It's me—in everything from picking a wife to picking a company for acquisition."[5] Mahoney's reference to "instinct" is a reference to the feeling function of judgment. He uses it but is sensitive to the fact that, in our culture, executives are not supposed to have feelings. There is a soft, mushy connotation to the word. In fact, feeling in the type model is a function of judgment that is opposed to thinking but equally valid.

Most of the misunderstanding centers around the confusion of unconscious, undifferentiated emotion and "affect" for conscious, differentiated feeling. Everyone has "feelings," but this use of the word often refers to unconscious as opposed to conscious feeling. It is difficult to adequately define feeling since the function is, in a fundamental way, completely opposed to thinking, and thinking is the function that is most closely linked to the development of language. Thus, thinking language is ill-suited and ultimately unable to describe feeling. The language of feeling is poetry, and it is noteworthy that poets in our society are few and far between. As with thinking, the degree to which a person's feeling function is differentiated is quite varied. For some, feeling is their superior or leading function. For others, it is their second, third, or fourth function.

Everyone recognizes that some people are more developed in their ability to think than others. What is equally true, but not equally recognized, is that some people are much more developed in their ability to feel. This does not mean that only feeling types have feelings, but rather that feeling types can deal with feelings directly and can consciously experience a broad range of them—"get in

[5]*Fortune* Magazine, April 23, 1979, p. 111.

touch with their feeling"—whereas those with less developed feelings will often face feeling indirectly.

Just as too much feeling can jam the circuits of a relationship, so can a lack of feeling boomerang. According to Gareth Wigan of The Ladd Company, Twentieth Century Fox caused the defection of Alan Ladd, Jr., Jay Kantor, and himself, plus the large group of talented people that followed them out of the lot—the group responsible for *Star Wars*, recipient of 33 Academy Awards and the largest single moneymaker in the industry's history—through lack of feeling. "The real reason the whole thing broke down at Fox," he says, "was because the management failed to understand the importance of human relationships, because of all the betrayals, not of us, but of other people in the division."[6]

It is interesting to note that so-called "woman's intuition" has never been proven to exist. There is, however, considerable evidence that women in general have a more developed feeling function, and the expression "woman's intuition" is a reference to a woman's ability to perceive and sense the feeling of others in a particular situation. Obviously, if your own feelings are not differentiated, you will not be able to perceive the feeling of others. If you don't have a differentiated function, you cannot assess that function in others. In other words, that whole side is blind. But if one develops the feeling function, and awareness of it, one can then have developed a capacity to perceive the feeling function in others.

Western culture has devoted an enormous amount of energy and effort so far in developing the thinking function in people. Although there is more emphasis today on development of the feeling function, this is still viewed

---

[6]Eliza G. C. Collins, "When Friends Run the Business," *Harvard Business Review*, July–August, 1980, pp. 87–99.

by most people as an activity of dubious and questionable value. The cultural attitude that surrounds and influences us is one that fails to appreciate the valid place of feeling as a function of judgment in life. Many people cannot even imagine what it would be like to experience differentiated feeling. They believe that it is "soft" and "mushy" and fail to appreciate that differentiated feeling is capable of making "hard" decisions. (Sidney' Carton's decision in Charles Dickens' *A Tale of Two Cities* to take the place of another at the guillotine was a feeling decision, but it certainly was a hard one.) The decision of many soldiers to lay down their lives for a friend is not only brave and heroic, but a hard decision. The difference between thinking and feeling judgments is not that one (thinking) is hard and that the other (feeling) is soft, but rather that thinking is objective and feeling is subjective.

Feeling, as a conscious function, is clear, reliable (it does not flip-flop around), and sensitive to reality (which means that feeling may be very tender and intimate), or it may be very "tough" and hard-nosed. Feeling is tough when it should be tough.

Example.   The CEO of one of the world's largest international organizations was noted for his sharp mind and quick thinking. Everything about him pointed to him as a man who operated primarily out of thinking and sensation. Theories and facts. Given this typological strength, you would expect the man to be *relatively* weak in the feeling function. This, in fact, was the case as was evidenced again and again in his career. One instance illustrates very well just how this weakness was expressed: An executive vice-president of his organization had, as a younger man, made an outstanding contribution to the organization. This was part of the history, or the collective memory, of the organization. Meanwhile, this man's first wife had died, and he had met and married a much younger woman. The second wife was very active socially, and the EVP did his best to keep up with her. He finally faltered, however, and had a heart attack on the dance floor one evening while boogying with his young wife. After this shocking experience, he decided that he needed to take it easier, so he started coming in to work at 11:00 AM and leaving at 2:30 PM after a two-hour lunch. This new work style created problems for the other vice-presidents in the organization, and there was pressure on the CEO to do something about this outrageous situation. However, the CEO could not bring himself to say anything to the executive vice-president. He said, whenever the matter was discussed, "If I say anything to X, it would kill him."

The CEO's feeling failed him in this situation. He was not tough enough to do what needed to be done, which was to sit down and talk to the executive vice-president about what was happening and do something about it. Thinking was no help at all, because there is no way that you can think yourself out of a situation like this. So the situation was "stuck." And it remained stuck.

This story illustrates how weak or unconscious feeling can trip up an otherwise competent executive. The other side of the coin is differentiated feeling. The sign of differentiated feeling is that it is reliable and clear. It may or may not be right. For example, the vice-president in charge of marketing at one large company said of his chairman, "I'm sure that at least 40 percent of his decisions are wrong, but, it doesn't matter. What matters is that he makes decisions, and you can't imagine the effect that this has on a large organization. It gives people a sense of direction and leadership that unleashes the latent energy and creativity of a large organization."

Professor Stan Davis of Boston University[7] makes the point that, in order to create organizations that respond to the intentions of people, it is necessary to manage the context, not the content. This means that it is necessary to see the whole and allow for contradictory approaches. To effectively manage the context, to create organizations that respond to intentions, it is essential to see the whole, and this is something that can only be done with intuition.

Example.   One person picks up an acorn and says, "here is an acorn." Another picks up an acorn and says, "here is an oak tree in the acorn stage of development." The person who sees only the acorn is seeing what exists right now and is sensing. The person who sees an oak tree in the acorn stage of development is also seeing the possibilities and is intuiting.

Organizations that respond to intentions require clear intentions to respond to. This is the beginning of organizational success. This is why it is absolutely crucial to address the questions: "What business are we in?" "Why are we here?" "What is the point of it all?" In order to answer these questions, there must be clear and differentiated feeling about what the point of it all is, and this feeling must be congruent with the values of the organizational members. This is one of the secret weapons of the Japanese: they forge organizations that are congruent with the values of the members. People share values and a sense of the meaning of life. If you examine the statements of Japanese business leaders

---

[7]John Poppy, "Between You and Me," interview with Stan Davis, *The Review*, November–December, 1981, p. 2.

on the purpose of the business, the first thing that stands out is that they all take the time to pronounce on their business and philosophy of life. They do this because they know that it is important to create a sense of purpose and a pool of shared values.

An important point to remember is that subjective feeling always enters into judgments, if not openly, then under the table, so to speak, disguised as thinking. One of the important contributions of the Jungian type model in improving the quality of decisions is its recognition and valuation of feeling. This recognition can bring feeling values out into the open, where they can be discussed, considered, and weighed against each other and against conclusions suggested by thinking. Whether we like it or not, feeling influences our thinking, and it will tend to focus or orient our perception. The more we get our feelings out and expressed, the more we are able to deal with feelings as facts in their own right, instead of feelings as distortion of our thoughts or perceptual focus.

OPPOSITION OF FUNCTIONS: CONSCIOUS AND UNCONSCIOUS

A fundamental fact about the mind is that the functions are in opposition. This is illustrated in Figure 1.3, where the perception functions, sensation and intuition, are opposed to each other like the judging functions, thinking and feeling. Thinking, when it is developed and active, tends to exclude feeling, and vice versa. Similarly, intuition is opposed to and excludes sensation, and vice versa. In the individual, this opposition of functions results in what can be described as an opposition of the conscious and unconscious functions. Thus, the conscious function is that which is customary, domi-

Figure 1.3. The four functions.

nant, habitual, primary, and leading. The unconscious function, which is opposed, is relatively undeveloped and undifferentiated, latent, repressed, and inferior. It is important to understand that this juxtaposition is relative: one person's unconscious intuition may be more effective than another's conscious intuition. The comparison is only made with regard to an individual psyche.

Figure 1.4 illustrates the opposition of functions and their relationship to each other. Thinking is shown at the top, in Panel A, to represent a person with superior thinking and inferior feeling. Panel B is rotated 180° to represent the opposite: superior feeling and inferior thinking. Panel C represents superior intuition, while Panel D, which is rotated 180°, shows superior sensation. Note that in each case the inferior or relatively

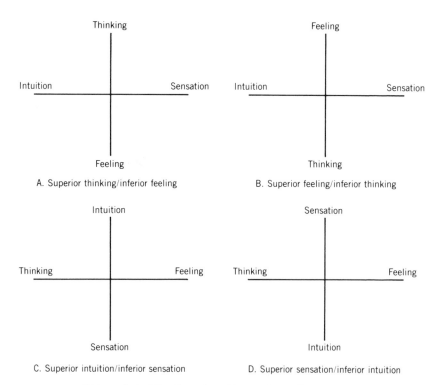

Figure 1.4. The four functions—four illustrations.

unconscious function is opposite the superior or conscious function.

If your predominant conscious function is either thinking or feeling, you are a judging type. If your predominant conscious function is either sensation or intuition, you are a perceptive type. Judging types, who relate to the world via thinking or feeling, typically prefer to live in a more planned, orderly way and want to regulate and control life. Perceptive types, who relate to the world via sensation or intuition, typically prefer to live in a more flexible, spontaneous way and want to understand life and adapt to it.

It would of course be ideal if each of us could fully utilize each of our functions and apply them as circumstances indicate. Unfortunately, in the differentiated or developed individual, this is extremely difficult to do. Jung himself believed that it is impossible. He said:

> There are individuals whose thinking and feeling are on the same level, both being of equal motive power for consciousness. But in these cases, there is also no question of a differentiated type, but merely a relatively undeveloped thinking and feeling. The *uniformly* conscious or *uniformly* unconscious state of the functions is, therefore, the mark of a primitive mentality.[8]

The concept of opposition is basic to Jung's theory, which began to form when he identified the first two functions—thinking (or "rational knowledge") and feeling—and realized that they were in opposition to each other. Also opposed is the other pair: sensation and intuition, as well as the attitudes; introversion and extroversion, although they are not mutually exclusive. Because one is predominantly extroverted, this does not mean that one can't also be somewhat introverted.

Jung held further that the hardest person to understand was the one with the same function—for example, feeling—but an opposite attitude. Thus, the extroverted feeler has the most trouble understanding the introverted feeler. Jung identified the concept of opposites "odd and even, above and below, good and evil" as the discovery of the Pythagoreans. One way of identifying your superior function is to infer it from an examination of the inferior or "missing" function. Thus, one infers "thinking" to be the superior function when one observes that in the individual, feeling is absent. A problem

[8]Jung, *Psychological Types*, p. 406.

arises, however, when an individual apparently displays a pair of opposed functions. One explanation is that the individual has consciously developed the inferior function in order to apply it to a task. Thus, an intuitive may consciously develop sensation as a survival tool in a sensation-dominated environment. To do this, to become aware of the inferior function, and, if appropriate, to access and develop it, can be a way of knowing and developing the individual's total potential.

In the end, the issue of whether or not the functions develop equally or in opposition, with the resulting consciousness and unconsciousness suggested by Jung, is an empirical rather than a theoretical issue. Clinical evidence suggests that in a normal person the unconscious function is partly conscious and available for use. But it is frequently true that its significance and potential are not fully recognized. For the neurotic, the unconscious function sinks almost wholly into the void. In this state, it is active, but in a negative way, giving rise to fantasies, complexes, and other psychological problems. It is not, in this totally unconscious state, accessible and available to the individual for appropriate use in adaptation to life.

THE INFERIOR FUNCTION

The inferior or unconscious function is our Achilles heel in life. It is particularly troublesome during periods of stress. For the intuitive, for example, whose unconscious function is sensation, there is the problem of forgetfulness under stress. The intuitive will often lose things, such as jewelry, wallets, passports, and umbrellas, or "forget" appointments and meetings. Intuition, on the other hand, is the unconscious function of the sensation type. Sensates see the "trees," that is, facts, but miss the forest. Their superior sense of the present, immediate reality often blinds them to the possibilities and potentials of a situation. In marketing, for example, the sensation function tends to miss new opportunities as it concentrates on data. On the other hand, the intuitive will often fail to recognize the nature of the existing opportunity.

For thinkers, the unconscious function is feeling. These people will often be out of touch with the individual needs and realities of superiors, subordinates, and peers—and themselves. The thinker is frequently experienced by others as tactless and self-absorbed. For the feeling type, the unconscious function is thinking. These types are highly sensitive to the atmosphere around them and to themselves but often fail to think things through and, as a consequence, are often controlled by thinkers.

There is often misunderstanding of Jung's "shadow" concept. Some view it as Freud did, as a sinister or "repressed" aspect of the psyche. Jung considered the development of consciousness as "the most precious fruit of the tree of knowledge," but he "recognized that without any doubt, the development of consciousness provided a seed for splitting the personality as a whole, of disassociating the superior and inferior parts of the personality."[9] Unlike Freud, Jung did not believe the inferior or unconscious part of the personality was repressed or free floating; he saw it instead as a part of the basic personality. He thought of it more as a "shadow." By shadow, he meant the "negative" side of the personality, or the sum of all those unpleasant qualities we like

[9]Liliane Frey-Rohn, *From Freud to Jung* (New York: Dell, 1974) p. 59.

to hide, together with the insufficiently developed functions and the content of the personal unconscious. Jung believed the shadow was "negative" only from the perspective of consciousness; it could be highly moral, but it was unknown to the conscious mind. Thus, says Frey-Rohn, "Jung . . . saw in it also the prospect of constructive seeds for future development.[10]

Much has been made in recent years of the connection between Jung's shadow or unconscious and his concept of "racial memory," the ancient paths in the psyche that lead back to our primitive beginnings and that can be accessed by artists and others through symbols and myths. In this role, the shadow connects the individual to his or her "racial"—(that is, human)—origins. Thus, the shadow should be valued as a source of hidden wisdom. In the case where the individual refuses absolutely to acknowledge the shadow, regarding it as evil, there would be a "black–white" split in which the individual would reject his or her unconscious and, as a consequence, exhibit neurotic symptoms. This agrees somewhat with Freud's idea about repression; the shadow is less differentiated and inferior to the consciousness, although, like the superior and conscious part of the psyche, it has ideas, thoughts, images, and value judgments. Thus, the shadow could be benign; it would only become pathological if repressed.

In the first part of life, the individual utilizes the conscious, superior part of the personality in order to deal with the demands of daily life. However, Jung believed that in later life the individual would find it necessary to integrate the shadow into the total personality in order to complete the psyche. Thus, we have the

[10]Ibid.

phenomenon of personality change in maturity (after 35, according to Jung), as hitherto latent talents, ideas, and interests surface in the personality. This capacity to connect with the collective unconscious—the opposite living dormant in the unconscious—would be the job of an integrated, fulfilled personality. Failure to do so would result in "severe disturbance." Jung saw the potential for renewal in liberation of the repressed shadow.

This concept of acceptance of both the conscious and the shadow aspects of the personality is, in Japan, considered to be an ideal basis for a relationship, both personal, as in marriage, and public, as at work. The Japanese value "compassion," which means to them an acceptance of the flaws in human nature. This is contrary to the Puritanism of Western society, with its endless fault-finding, which is intolerant of weaknesses or flaws, and which demands that "negative" traits be hidden. One aspect of this is the so-called superwoman complex, in which the American career woman has to be at once the perfect mother, wife, and executive, and is so portrayed in the media. As writers are correctly pointing out, this image of superwoman or superman (the successful executive, playboy, husband, father, etc.) is destructive to real people who cannot possibly live up to these ideals. To have "compassion," in the Japanese sense, is a source of strength for Japanese people who feel that they will be accepted even if they are not perfect. It is one of the reasons that Japanese corporations are able to hold the loyalty of their workers. Another subtle thought, according to Professor Yuji Aida of the University of Kyota, is the idea of consideration, the "perception, sympathy and modesty not to impose a burden on another. It is a condition of neither attachment nor separation."

"Shadows," says Professor Aida, "are no more than a lack of light."[11] It is important to accept—to "cast light" on the shadows. In other words, if you want to develop a latent function, you need to put light on it.

THE RELATIONSHIP OF FUNCTIONS TO THE UNCONSCIOUS

The functions are the ways in which the mind or psyche perceives and judges. The relationship of the functions to the unconscious is shown in Figure 1.5, which is a representation of an individual with superior thinking and auxiliary intuition. Notice that the function in Figure 1.5 which is closest to the unconscious is feeling.

Figure 1.6 represents a person with superior intuition. Notice that in this figure the function which is closest to the unconscious is sensation. The outer ring in each of these illustrations represents the leading role of the conscious function, which is that function the individual uses primarily to deal with life in general and work in particular. The fourth function, which is the opposite of the first, is the least differentiated or developed, and the one that is closest to the unconscious.

Example.   A case of an intuitive (represented by Figure 1.6) who had little sensation is suggested by the behavior of William Lear, the late aircraft designer. Although he was a genius at design, we know that he had absolutely no interest in legal documents, which are full of detail and require the use of sensation. Before he died, Lear signed a number of documents that directed his

[11]Yuji Aida, "The Need to Be Convinced: Theory of a Paradox," *Look Japan*, December 10, 1979, pp. 8–9.

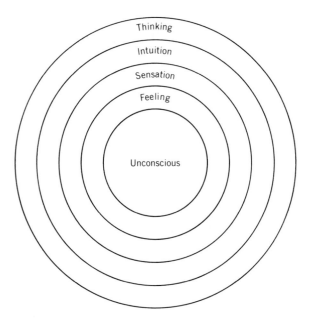

Figure 1.5. Superior thinking/auxiliary intuition/inferior feeling.

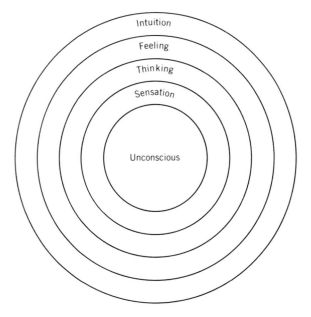

Figure 1.6. Superior intuition/auxiliary feeling/inferior sensation.

company to continue work on the next generation of Lear jets. His heirs, concerned that his estate would be consumed by the new project, sued to get control of his estate. One of the issues in the lawsuit was the question of whether or not the documents he signed expressed his real intentions because he *never read them.*

This is characteristic behavior for a highly developed intuitive person with little or no interest in exercising sensation, which might be largely undifferentiated and unconscious—at least on the surface.

AUXILIARY FUNCTIONS: DIFFERENT BUT NOT OPPOSED

In addition to the conscious function and the unconscious function, there is the auxiliary function, one that exerts a codetermining influence on the way the individual relates to the world. The auxiliary function is different from the conscious function but not opposed to it. Thus, conscious thinking as a primary function can pair with either intuition or sensation as the auxiliary, but never with feeling, because thinking is opposed to feeling. Conscious intuition could pair with either thinking or feeling, but not with sensation, because sensation is opposed to intuition. Therefore, if the conscious function is a perceptive function, the auxiliary function will be a decision-making or judging function, or vice versa.

The remaining function is the third function. It is not wholly conscious, unconscious, or auxiliary, and it is best identified via a process of elimination. Unlike the unconscious function, the third function is available. The hallmark of this function is the greater effort required to bring it to bear. For example, the intuitive or sensate feeler's third function is thinking. These people can think, but must make an effort. Their natural and more comfortable response to life is through perception and feeling.

The conscious and unconscious nature of the functions is not an absolute or comparative measure such as I.Q. An individual with conscious sensation and unconscious intuition may very well have a more creative, effective, and reliable intuition than another less-able person who has conscious intuition and unconscious sensation.

FOUR STYLES OF MANAGEMENT

There have been over the years literally hundreds of management-style typologies offered to explain the different "styles" of managing. Most of these typologies incorporate the four Jungian functions as a major element of organizing observed styles of managing. One of the most popular management-style typologies is the driving, expressive, amiable, and analytical style-model. These styles and their relationship to the Jungian functions are shown below:

1. **Driving Style.** This is the manager who gets the job done in the most practical and efficient manner while controlling all aspects of the activity. (This style is closely linked to the sensation function. A manager with a driving style would be a manager with a highly differentiated sensation function.)

2. **Expressive Style.** This is the management style that gets the job done with enthusiasm and excitement, using hunches and opinions to react to

immediate demands. (This style is closely linked to the intuitive function. A manager operating with this style would have a highly differentiated intuitive function.)

3. **Amiable Style.** This manager gets the job done cooperatively by getting the entire team equally involved and participating in team activity. (This style is closely linked to the feeling function. A manager operating with this style would have a highly differentiated feeling function.)

4. **Analytical Style.** This manager gets the job done with logical analysis and problem solving, using all available facts and data. (This style is closely linked to the thinking function. A manager operating with this style would have a highly differentiated thinking function.)

REFERENCES

Hall, Calvin S. and Vernon J. Nordby. *A Primer of Jungian Psychology.* New York: Mentor, 1973.

de Laszlo, Violet Staub, Ed. *The Basic Writings of C. G. Jung.* New York: The Modern Library, 1959.

Campbell, Joseph, Ed. *The Portable Jung.* New York: The Viking Press, 1971.

C. G. Jung, *Psychological Types.* In *The Collected Works of C. G. Jung,* Vol. 6, Bollingen Series 20. Princeton: Princeton University Press, 1976. (Originally published in German as *Psychologische Typen,* Zurich: Rascher Verlag, 1921).

von Franz, Marie-Louise, and James Hillman. *Lectures on Jung's Typology,* Zurich: Spring Publications, 1971.

2

Are You What You Think You Are?

In every adult there lurks a child—an eternal child, something that is always becoming, is never completed, and calls for unceasing care, attention, and education. That is the part of the human personality which wants to develop and become whole.

C. G. JUNG

This chapter focuses on how you got to be the type you are today. As you will soon see, we do not all develop according to our innate types. One of the major conclusions of type research is that many people are living in a state of what could be called type falsification. How can this be?

STAGES OF LIFE AND TYPE

There are three stages in the development of type in an individual's life. The first is the initial stage, when the dominant attitude of the child is recognizable. This is a crucial stage and one in which sensitivity to individual character can have profound significance to future development.

The second stage of development is from young adulthood to midlife, when we control and suppress one or more functions to achieve success and adaptation in the academic and business world. In our sensation-oriented, thinking culture, this often means suppressing intuition and feeling.

The third stage of development occurs at midlife when we begin to pay more attention to recognizing suppressed or relatively undervalued functions. This can be a very turbulent stage in life, as anyone over 35 can testify. For example, conflict in marriage may develop when one partner begins to exercise functions that were previously left to the other marriage partner. It is also a time of career change when many people redefine their goals and management or professional style to reflect functions that may not have been adequately valued and expressed in the first half of life. In general, if your development in the first half of life focused on thinking and sensation, you will probably begin to rely increasingly on intuition and feeling. This is especially true of intuition, which is a function that draws on life experience. As there is more experience, there is more to draw on. If early development focused on feeling and intuition, you may feel a strong need to develop thinking and sensation. In marriages where the man worked and the woman raised children, often at midlife the man gets in touch with his feelings while the woman starts a career. Each is developing a neglected side of his or her psyche.

FALSIFICATION OR REVERSAL OF TYPE

Type characteristics are inherited or genetically imprinted rather than learned. This conclusion is based on the frequent occurrence of different typology in identical twins raised in the same home, and on the fact that children often exhibit type characteristics very early in life that are different from their parents. Indeed, there is a widespread incidence of falsification or reversal of type. These cases occur when a child is raised by parents in an environment that is insensitive to the child's character and when the child responds by adopting attitude or function preferences other than his or her innate attitude or function preferences. For example, a child might be a feeling, intuitive type born into a family with a tradition of academic achievement. If such a child is encouraged to excel academically as a thinker, he or she may adapt to life primarily with the thinking function. This, of course, would be enormously supported and encouraged by the wider culture, especially for male children. Since thinking and feeling are opposed, this falsification or reversal results in suppression of the innate superior or preferred function. This may work rather well during the first half of life, but as a person gets older, alienation from the innate function leads to increasing feelings of inner conflict, tension, and neurosis.

Other evidence supporting the theory that type is inherited is research on the human brain. Originally, the theory was that the brain was infinitely malleable and a nerve in the brain could connect as readily to one place as to another, like the wiring in a house. It was thought that the brain had to learn what to do. Today, the theory that the brain is hard-wired from birth by genetic forces is widely accepted.

In addition, clinical experience of psychoanalysts, some of whom use the type theory in diagnosing patients, shows that patients in therapy often discover they have been adapting to life with their second, third, or even fourth functions. When they "discover" their true superior function, a marked improvement in effectiveness and an overall sense of well-being often results.

PERSONAL GROWTH: A TYPOLOGICAL PERSPECTIVE

If you have adapted to life with a false primary function, that is to say, if you believe, based on your experience, that the function you rely on in your profession is not your superior function, then you are working and living in a false type situation. This presents an opportunity to (1) discover your true innate superior function, and (2) begin to rely on and use that function in your work. If you do this, you will discover that the function you have left relatively unused will begin to develop and grow, and you will experience a sense of personal growth, development, and satisfaction as you begin to rely on your true strength rather than a second, third, or even fourth function.

Expectations play an important role in changing behavior and capability. What we expect to do or happen usually happens. This is illustrated in a striking way by the experience of C. S. Lewis, author of *The Screwtape Letters*. Lewis has described his long, creative immersion in *The Screwtape Letters*, a book that made Lewis rich and famous. His immersion in the psyche of the devil, Screwtape, caused him to think continually of "evil, rot, decay, negativism and ruin." The mental exercise, he reports, literally made him mentally ill.

Lewis had become what he thought! He had become what he said! The only solution seemed to be to think, save, and write his way out of the twilight of depression into a condition of mental health and wholeness. The result was *Surprised by Joy*, and when he wrote it, he became vigorous and optimistic once more. Commitment springs from expectations. Commitments that are fulfilled create new and stronger expectations.

The expectation of what is possible is found in what we actually do. Typologically, one of the ways we develop and grow as we get older is that we expect more from the sacrificed inferior functions that had been pushed aside in the first half of life in order to get established. As these functions are recognized and encouraged to develop through activity (study, group activities, exercises), the expectation is fulfilled by their activation. Jung established "maturity" at age 35. We live longer now, and youth is prolonged. Thus people may enter the creative life before 40, but the period of greatest creativity in the United States is generally thought to be between 40 and 60. People like Henry Ford and Andrew Carnegie did not really achieve until they reached 40.

An example of a midlife change is Byron Donzis, a talented intuitive inventor, who, in middle age, was "converted" by bankruptcy to paying attention to financial, practical, "sensation" considerations. Making a 180° turn on his previous perspective, which was totally concerned with creativity, he concentrated on learning how a businessperson's mind works. "It's like watching a diesel locomotive, I don't want to look like him or sound like him, but I'm not going to stand in his way." Donzis is now not only a talented inventor, which he always was, but he is also a successful businessman who is reaping financial rewards by applying intuition *and* sensation to his work.

THE IMPORTANCE OF SELF-KNOWLEDGE: HOW TO AVOID BECOMING "JUST A TYPE"

For management, the most important implication of the theory of psychological types is its potential for creating greater self-awareness and self-knowledge. The more we know about ourselves, the greater the chance that we will act in ways that increase our consciousness and capacity to live our lives in ways that have value and meaning to us. If you discover, as you learn about type, that you are a thinker with unconscious feeling, this is knowledge that you can use to enrich your life by taking steps to develop your unconscious feelings. If you discover that you are an intuitive, you can take steps to develop your sensation. Similarly, if you are a feeling type, you can focus on your thinking; if you are a sensate, you can focus on your intuition.

At the same time, knowledge of type will give you a basis for more fully appreciating types who are different from you. You may, as a thinking sensate, have always looked down on the creative, intuitive, feeling types. With knowledge of type, this should no longer happen. Now you should know that there is no such thing as a good or bad type. To fully and adequately perceive and judge, we need both forms of perception and both functions of judgment, as well as both attitudes. If any of the functions or either of the attitudes is not expressed, there is danger that something vital will be overlooked.

This does not mean that you, as a manager, must become a person for all seasons. It simply means that the organization must reflect each of the functions and both of the attitudes. In order for this to happen, people with type strength in each of the functional areas must be recruited, and each of the types must be valued and respected for the contribution it makes to the work of the organization.

If you aspire to the ranks of senior management in your company or organization, you must become typologically conscious in each of the four functions. You will need feeling to relate to your staff and to build your organization; you will need sensation to get the facts; you will need thinking to sort out the logical conclusions that flow from the facts of the situation; and you will need intuition to foresee the future situation.

If you look at the truly effective managers, the ones who have risen to the top of well-managed companies and who themselves have contributed to the growth and development of their organizations, you are looking at managers who are relatively evenly developed. If this is not the case, you're looking at managers who have no difficulty in appreciating each of the types. The current CEO of one of America's best-managed companies, for example, is a clear thinking/sensate style manager, just as the CEOs of this company have always been. However, in spite of this strong bias toward thinking and sensation, he has hired and promoted some of the most intuitive managers in American business. This is truly a sign of greatness in management.

Another highly effective CEO of a smaller, highly regarded company is a feeling/sensate type. However, this man is an excellent thinker and is very open to new ideas both within and without his organization. The strength of this manager is the strength of a person who is not wearing blinders to important dimensions of reality. The effective executive must see both the present and the future (i.e., what is coming over the hill) and she or he must be able to judge and make choices. Effective judgment requires good thinking and feeling. The importance of thinking to judgment is widely accepted, but the importance of feeling is equally necessary. Without differentiated feeling ability, the executive will be unable to act consistently and reliably in the areas where thinking does not provide the answers.

Benjamin Rosen sold his highly successful newsletter on the electronics industry and took a job as CEO of a

Table 2.1. Frequency of Types

	Center for Application of Psychological Types Data Bank[1]	Wharton Business School Students[2]	George Washington University M.B.A. Candidates[3]	Division Managers—A Large U.S. Multinational Corporation[4]
Extroverts	53%	70%	64%	55%
Introverts	47	30	36	45
Superior Intuition	30	19	23	16
Superior Sensation	16	28	16	3
Superior Thinking	24	38	32	68
Superior Feeling	30	15	29	13

[1]75,745 cases collected between 1970 and 1976. *Data Source:* MBTI News, Volume 1, Number 1, 1976. Center for Application of Psychological Types, 1976.

[2]488 cases. *Data Source:* Myers, Isabel Briggs, the *Myers-Briggs Type Indicator Manual,* Palo Alto, California, Consulting Psychologists Press, 1962. Table D-5.

[3]69 cases, February, 1978. Degree Candidates in Business Policy Course. *Data Source:* Myers-Briggs Type Indicator.

[4]31 cases, February 1978. *Data Source:* Myers-Briggs Type Indicator.

small computer company. His comment about this experience is that it is "very humbling" because he has found that one analyzes all aspects of a problem and then decides on the basis of gut feeling. What Rosen learned is that managing a business requires the whole brain (sensation, intuition, thinking, and feeling), whereas the creating of a newsletter can be based on perception and analysis (sensation, intuition, and thinking). This is what M.B.A.s are not taught in business school because it is difficult to teach people how to feel in a classroom.

FREQUENCY OF TYPES IN THE POPULATION

A number of instruments have been developed to determine a person's psychological type. The most widely used of these is the Myers-Briggs Type Indicator (MBTI).

Unfortunately, research to date has not been addressed to random population samples, so it is not possible to report for the population at large the results obtained from the MBTI indicator. Table 2.1 presents frequency of type data for four nonrandom groups. The first column reports the frequency for 75,745 cases collected between 1970 and 1976 by the Center for Applications of Psychological Types. The second, third, and fourth columns of the table present data for Wharton Business School students, George Washington University M.B.A. candidates, and division managers of a large U.S. multinational corporation.

A comparison of the data bank with the students and practicing managers suggests the following tentative hypotheses:

1.   Business school students and managers are significantly more extroverted than the population at large.

2. Business school students and practicing managers represent a disproportionately larger percentage of the thinkers in the population and a disproportionately smaller percentage of intuitives and feelers.

It is significant that the George Washington University M.B.A. candidates reflect relatively high scores on the feeling function. This is accounted for in part by the larger number of women in the George Washington University sample, and also by a cultural shift that is giving increasing value and weight to the expression of feeling as opposed to thinking judgment.

Another major problem of determining type frequency in any population is the limitation of the test instrument itself. In addition to the problems of people reacting individually to test questions, there is also the problem of inadequate self-knowledge and type reversal. More research needs to be done to determine the incidence of the various types in the population and to identify individuals who do not know their own type and who will confound any attempt to measure their innate type characteristics.

The reason it is so difficult to establish typology for people is the very healthy tendency and instinct in everyone to compensate and maintain equilibrium. If a person is weak in a function or attitude, he or she will naturally try to compensate for this. The compensation may result, particularly if it is encouraged by cultural factors, in the person actually being confused about his or her own nature.

3

Shifting Gears: How to Change

Firepower, Mobility, and Shock Action

THE MOTTO OF UNITED STATES ARMY ARMOR

One of the most important aspects of typological development is the capacity to "shift gears" and move from one function to the next in the process of perceiving and arriving at judgments and decisions. The inability to "shift" from one function to another is a clear symptom of arrested typological development. You can get by on one or two functions in many situations, but effectiveness is limited because one or two functions usually do not fully comprehend all of the important elements of the situation. In this chapter, the dynamics of type functioning are described, and some of the implications of rigid type functioning are discussed.

DYNAMIC INTERACTION

The functions do not operate or exist in isolation, but rather in dynamic interactive relation to each other. A typical sequence is that in which background data are acquired through sensate perception. These data become the background field for intuitive perceptions about the nature of the whole and about possible futures, or what might be, as opposed to what is. The combination of these two function perceptions is the basis for judgments that can be drawn from thinking, that is, inductive or deductive logic, or from feeling, that is, an individual's own subjective values.

Another sequence of dynamic interaction begins with a feeling, an aesthetic value; from that, the gathering of data; then the analysis of these data with thinking; and finally the arrival at judgments and choices out of feeling and thinking. If the feeling is the beginning, it orients the perception of facts. The scientist who discovered Valium, the largest selling drug in history, began with an aesthetic feeling about crystal structure and followed that feeling choice to the discovery of Valium.

Another example of dynamic interaction is found in the choice of vocation or career. What do you want to do with your life? The answer to this question might begin with perception: What is out there? How do people make a living? How do people make a contribution? Here, much of the perception is sensation perception of the facts: What does a surgeon do? How much does he or she earn? What training is required to become one? Beyond these bare facts, intuition can look behind the facts to get a sense of what it is like to be a surgeon, what the future of the profession might be, what it would be like to be in medical school, what it would be like to be in residency, what the chances are of getting admitted to medical school or to a surgical residency. In other words, you might begin with perception, then, with facts and your own intuitive sense of what is out there, you could analyze the data logically to think about risk, reward, and effort. Next you could draw on your feeling of what you want to do with your life. Feeling is obviously a key function in this decision-making process.

THE MASTER INVESTORS: HOW ATTITUDE AND FUNCTION INTERACT

A master investor is someone who has demonstrated over a variety of markets the ability to perform, that is, to make money. The hot shots who score because they are riding a current fad are excluded by definition from the category—to be included, the individual must have made money over a variety of market conditions. In order to qualify, a person must be a realist. Investing is reality, both present and future. Anyone who has a tendency to fantasize or live off wishes or delusions will be found out sooner or later in the investment game.

Typologically, this quality, realism, is both extroversion and introversion. The master investor is a person who is reliably connected to each of these attitudes. Extroversion is needed to connect to collective attitudes toward value. Markets shift from an optimistic emphasis on current and expected earnings to prices that are based on an estimate of a company's worth—that is, from the income statement to the balance sheet. Extroversion, the outer orientation, connects an investor to this reality.

Introversion is needed to be oriented by an inner sense of value. If there is only extroversion, the investor will very likely be blown away by the current fashion and get caught short like all of the other lemmings who only follow the collective judgment about value. To succeed as a master investor, one needs to have an inner sense of value, to stay with that inner sense, and to act on it, because the master investor is always buying and selling from the crowd. When the master buys, the market is selling. When the master sells, the market is buying. The essential quality of the master is that he or she knows what the market is thinking and what its values are, and also has a standpoint, so that he or she has the guts to buy and sell against the collective belief. The application of the two attitudes in perceiving reality is extroverted sensation and intuition, and introverted sensation and intuition. This is especially true for extroverted sensation and introverted intuition. If you think about it, these two functions and attitudes are the opposite sides of a coin. Extroverted sensation and introverted intuition, when really developed, fully support and complement each other. Extroverted sensation will feed introverted intuition. It will provide a rich background of facts, figures, and data that the introverted intuition can synthesize in arriving at an intuitive perception. Similarly, introverted intuition can guide and direct extroverted sensation. What kind of facts and data are you going to collect? Whether you admit it or not, you are guided by something when you perceive some fact or aspect of life. Your intuition will, either consciously, or unconsciously if you let it be unconscious, put you in one direction or another because selectivity in the perception of information is essential. We must be selective for two reasons: (1) there is far more information than we can ever absorb, and (2) our capacity to absorb information is limited. We could not, even if we wanted to, take in all of the information available.

A master investor has other qualities. First, he or she

is intelligent and dedicated to his or her craft. The master investor invests as a vocation. He or she always rejoices in his or her vocation. Evidence of this are long hours, and the twinkle in the eye when this person talks about work. Second, the master investor is disciplined and patient. If you know that you are right, it is not hard to wait. How do you know that you're right? If you have really done your homework, you know. If you don't know, you will be shaken out at precisely the wrong moment. Third, the master investor is a loner. This means that he or she is an introvert when push comes to shove. This must be. If, when push came to shove, he or she were an extrovert, he or she would, by definition, go with the collective. The master investor perhaps gives us an expanded sense of what is meant by the term "introvert." It puts the term into a positive light, for we can see that one must have this quality in order to be truly successful in investing and in almost any other field. If, for example, your field is design and you simply give people what they now have, chances are you will be left behind by other designers who offer something new, something that catches the public eye. This talent for catching the eye of the public or the target market, is one of knowing where people are now and trusting your own intuition about where they will be and what they will like tomorrow. Guessing about what they will go for tomorrow is taking a risk, and it requires that the decision-maker be, in the moment of the decision, a loner, or typologically, an introvert.

WHY DO EXECUTIVES AND MANAGERS MISPERCEIVE REALITY?

If we are equipped with sensate and intuitive perception functions, why is there so much misperception of reality? There are a number of reasons. First, decision-makers (DMs) tend to fit incoming information into their existing theories and images. Typologically, DMs don't actually see the world as it is. What they see is really a projection of their own inner theory, idea, or image. For years, U.S. executives could not see that the Japanese were doing it better. Instead, what they saw were foreign-looking people smiling and bowing, and saying yes to everything. They were people who lost World War II, people who lived in paper houses. They were not to be taken seriously. This is not perception; it is projection.

Another example of this problem is the international economy. It is quite clear that any company wishing to survive in an industry that can be entered by companies located outside the home country must recognize the possibility that one day it will be competing in world markets with companies located all over the world. In other words, in order to survive, its strategy must take into account the reality of an international economic order. In fact, many companies still operate in the illusion of the national economy.

Many of the most powerful business tools and concepts are really guides to perception. A good example is the marketing concept, a maxim that says the customer is the person or organization that puts bread on your table. Therefore, the customer must be the focus of your effort: you are in business to create and to hold customers, and you must accept and recognize this fact. This is an image of what you are in business for, and, if you hold and accept this image, you will take in information about the customer, you will listen to your customer, and you will be sensitive to your customer. You will, if you are good at what you do and you work very hard at it, serve your customer better than your competitors and prosper in the process.

An example of a maxim that is responsible for misperception of reality is the "bottom line." You have heard the expression, "the ultimate test in this organization is the bottom line," that is, the bottom line of the profit and loss statement, or the *reported* net profit. This is a theory that holds that what really will make things better, what really will work, is for management to focus its attention on the bottom line. Keep in mind that this is not focusing on the customer, nor is it focusing on the people in the organization who make things happen—it is focusing on the "bottom line." This is an example of a theory leading to a serious misperception of reality. The real bottom line is the customer who puts bread on the table and the people in the organization who make everything happen. The bottom line is a consequence, not a cause. The bottom line maxim shifts management's attention from causes to consequences and the result is as you would expect. The short-run reported "bottom line" is excellent, but the longer-run health and even survival of the business is undermined.

No one can live without a theory or image, so I am not proposing that as a result of reading this book, or of any other experience, the reader can go out and perceive reality. What I am suggesting is that everyone should recognize that theories and images determine what we see, and that we all need to carefully assess our theories. What are they? What is it that orients us? Do our theories correspond to reality? Unless you have good reason to believe otherwise, I suggest that you try to orient yourself by the theory that the customer is the basis for your survival, that your competitor is the person you must beat in serving your customers, that your competitors and customers are part of a global system, and that you are also part of that system. The key words in this description of reality are: marketing concept/customer focus, competitive analysis, and international strategy and plan.

A second reason for the frequent misperception of reality among DMs is that they are apt to err in being too wedded to the established view and too closed to new information, as opposed to being too willing to alter their theories. This hypothesis translates into type as follows: too often people lead from judgment instead of being open to information that might modify their theories about how things are. For example, a division of a large U.S. multinational corporation is a world leader in supplying customers with antennae for both radio and TV broadcasting. In addition, the division has a strong position in supplying customers with resale items that fill out a customer's need for broadcast equipment. So far, so good. Several years ago, the chairman of the company remarked that he thought the division had a great opportunity to get into the TV camera business. At that time, the division decided to go after a position in that area. Today, the division has a leading position in broadcast antennae and in resale items for broadcasters, but it is a weak last in the TV camera market. What has happened in this division is that it is throwing good money after bad in a futile attempt to do something that cannot be done. A realistic assessment of its strengths and weaknesses, vis-à-vis its competitors in this market, would leave no room for doubt that it makes no sense to keep trying to establish a position in this market. The division will always be a day late and a dollar short vis-à-vis its competitors, who are more solidly positioned in this particular business by right of their technology, share manufacturing, research focus, and resources.

The essence of the superior manager is his or her ability to withhold judgment and to make decisions. There is a paradox here: the ability to make decisions is the ability to suspend perception and to judge. But the ability to perceive reality, as opposed to the misperception of reality, is based on the ability to suspend judgment and to remain open to evidence, and to what is, in fact, real. One of the absolutely essential characteristics of the world today, yesterday, and tomorrow is that it changes. The world is constantly changing, and to get stuck with a theory or image is truly to be not of this world, but to be dead. To be in the past is not reality; it is a memory, and not a memory of how it "actually" was, but only how it seemed to the person whose memory is adjusted by time.

Beyond being aware that being too closed is a major danger, is there anything that can be done? Fortunately, the answer is yes. First, recognize that you do not take in information like some kind of a cosmic truth machine. Your perception is organized and filtered through your theories and images, so the more you know about these theories and images, the more you will know about reality, as opposed to the misperception that supports you in place of judgment.

Second, make your assumptions as explicit as possible. Put these assumptions out for critical review and evaluation. When the information comes in, see how it relates to the assumptions. As an example of how not to proceed, consider the investor who decided to buy an oil stock because he read an article in *Forbes* about the value of the reserves of a major oil company. He bought the company's stock because: (1) he believed that the stock was worth the per-share value of its reserves, (2) he believed that the market would soon recognize reserve asset value as a new basis for valuing all oil stocks, (3) he had seen a number of stories on the reserve asset value of the reserves of major oil and mineral companies, and (4) he believed that these stories would change the way that investors value oil company stocks. Notice that these assumptions are all based on belief: there is no evidence here of what investors will do, or even what they currently believe. There are no extroverted data here. Therefore, the decision to buy is one-sided, and, because it is based only on introverted belief, it is dangerous, at least in the short run. Needless to say, this investor lost a good deal of money and was poorer but wiser from the experience.

TYPE AND LISTENING

One of the ways the type model can make a difference in your life is to support you in your listening. Listening is a key to having any influence at all in a group, whether it be with a friend, in your family, or at work. Effective listening requires the active engagement of each function. Therefore, no matter what your function preference is, listening is difficult because it requires the active use of the inferior function. Intuitives have a difficult time listening because it requires the use of their fourth function, sensation. This is always a real chore. If you are an intuitive, recognize that you are going to have to make a huge effort to listen whenever you have to take in facts and details. When an intuitive gets sleepy at meetings, conferences, or even when talking on a one-to-one basis, he or she is becoming unconscious. This happens when such a person is faced with the need to draw on the fourth function. There is no easy solution to this problem. Knowing this is what is happening may help the intuitive muster the energy to keep him- or herself conscious, which is another way of saying that one must keep one's inferior function active. If one stays awake and alert, what one is doing is pulling one's fourth function from the unconscious into the conscious sphere.

Thinkers must make a special effort to listen with active feeling. If feeling is unconscious, much of the content in what someone is trying to say will be missed. For example, if someone is trying to say something about how he or she feels about a matter, this message will only come through on a feeling level. Again, a sure sign that you are tuning someone out is lack of interest, boredom, and, of course, falling asleep or getting drowsy.

Feelers must make their effort to listen to the ideas and theories that are always part of the message of the thinker. While it is true that there is no idea that will fully and completely explain any specific situation, it is also true that without ideas (theories) we are left in chaos. Ideas are essential for making sense out of the chaos of reality, and it is important to listen to the idea or belief or theory of the thinker.

Sensates must make special effort to listen to the ideas and fantasies of the intuitive. This is difficult because the tendency of the sensate is not to hear the intuitive idea. It is not concrete, it lacks substance, and it often seems totally worthless and valueless. It takes a special effort to listen and register an intuitive idea. This effort is one of the reasons that advertising agencies exist. Clients could do their own advertising and save the commission, but clients would have difficulty in creating an environment where creative people were free to, and encouraged to, do their best work.

MANAGEMENT

As all experienced managers know, management cannot be taught. In spite of the fact that we have schools, courses, and books on the subject, management is a matter of experience, common sense, and the right attitude, none of which can be taught in a classroom. A manager must make work challenging and rewarding so that people will remain in the organization for many years. Nothing can be accomplished when there is constant turnover of people because the organization does not benefit from the accumulation of experience and "corporate" memory.

Managers must instill an attitude of personal responsibility for seeing that jobs are accomplished. Managers must also be concerned with details because if they don't think they are important no one else will either. Managers must concern themselves with the future because if they don't think about the future neither will their subordinates.

To maintain proper control, managers must know what is going on. There are many ways of doing this, and all, according to Retired Admiral Hyman G. Rickover, involve "constant drudgery."[1] This drudgery is the drudgery of pulling out the inferior function when you would rather be doing what comes easily. If you are an intuitive, you would rather be concentrating on planning and the future at the expense of the present reality. If you are a sensate, you would rather be concentrating on the present reality at the expense of the future. If you are a thinker, you would rather concentrate on plans and designs, as opposed to the people who are going to make things happen. If you are a feeler, you would rather concentrate on people at the expense of needed plans and designs. Thus, management is a skill that demands the exercise of type dynamics. No matter where you start on the typological wheel, you must go around to the difficult inferior side if you are going to be an effective manager. This means, sad to say, that to be a truly

[1]Hyman G. Rickover, "Getting the Job Done Right," *The New York Times*, November 25, 1981, p. A25.

effective manager, most people will find it necessary to live through and experience more than a little drudgery. One of the things that identifies someone with the real potential and capacity to manage is his or her tolerance for accepting this drudgery, which is another way of saying that the person must have the capacity to draw not only on superior function, but also on inferior function.

According to Ralph Z. Sorenson, President and Chief Executive Officer of Barry Wright Corporation, the ability to make positive things happen most distinguishes the successful from the mediocre or unsuccessful manager. "It is far better to have dependable managers who can make the right things happen in a timely fashion than to have brilliant, sophisticated, highly educated executives who are excellent at planning, analyzing, and dissecting, but who are not so good at implementing. The most cherished manager is one who says 'I can do it,' and then does."[2]

Planning, analyzing, and dissecting are skills that require thinking. This can be taught and learned at school. Managing requires the use of feeling, intuition, and sensation in addition to thinking. These functions are best developed and exercised by experience.

[2]Ralph Z. Sorenson, "A Lifetime of Learning to Manage Effectively," *The Wall Street Journal*, February 26, 1983.

4

Communication Styles

We simply have to develop better methods of communication with the people.

ADLAI E. STEVENSON

INTRODUCTION

Have you ever wondered why it is so difficult to talk with or get through to some people and so easy to talk with others? Have you ever found, when you are getting nowhere in trying to express your point in a conversation, that a change of approach "gets through" to the other person? These experiences are classic symptoms of communications obstacles created when the sender is operating in one function and the receiver is operating in another.

It is widely agreed that one of the main reasons for the difficulty in communicating is the failure to see things from the other person's point of view. A classic example of this fact is the miscommunication between Lord Raglan and Lord Lucan at the Battle of Balaklava:

> At the Battle of Balaklava Lord Raglan sent a message to Lord Lucan, telling him to attack the enemy guns. From where he was, on a hilltop, it was perfectly clear what he meant. Down in a valley Lord Lucan had a different view of the battlefield, which did not include the cannon which Lord Raglan wanted to recapture, but did include whole batteries to which he had not meant to refer. On Lucan's orders, Lord Cardigan charged them at the head of the Light Brigade, which was totally destroyed. The point to emphasize is that Lord Raglan, who had many virtues, lacked the imagination (intuition) needed to realize what the battlefield looked like from a different angle and indeed on a different level. This sort of mistake is repeated every day and is always the result of a failure to see the situation from someone else's point of view.[1]

When you are attempting to communicate, always remember the fate of poor Lord Cardigan. First, don't assume that you are communicating unless there is visible evidence that your audience is listening. It is easy to tell when an audience is not receiving your message: people are falling asleep, they have a glazed look in the eyes or their eyes roll in their head, or they are getting up and leaving. This is embarrassing, even painful, but very clear. If this is happening, ask yourself, "Do I have something to say?" If the answer is no, that should be the end of it. Cut your losses, go home, and figure out if you do have something to say. If the answer to this question is "yes," then you may have a problem with your communication style.

[1]C. Northcote Parkinson, *The Law* (Boston: Houghton Mifflin, 1980), p. 203.

THINKING STYLE

Thinkers, for example, are interested in impersonal analysis of cause and effect. They are not likely to be convinced by anything but logic and reason. They live according to a formula that embodies their basic understanding of the world. Any change in their life requires a change of the formula, and any effective communication requires the taking of this formula into account. To persuade the thinker, one needs a logically sound and convincing plan.

FEELING STYLE

Feelers tend to be warm and enthusiastic and judge everything by personal values. To communicate with a feeling type, it is necessary to first establish rapport. This requires time. Feeling types are notorious for their enjoyment, and indeed for their need, of talk. It takes a special effort for them to be brief and businesslike. To communicate with the feeler, one has to concentrate on establishing rapport and on being sensitive to the feeler's personal likes and dislikes.

SENSING STYLE

Those who perceive with their sensing function are practical, realistic, factual, and very concerned with the here and now. To persuade a sensation type, you must focus on the facts of the present situation.

INTUITIVE STYLE

The intuitive is an imaginative, future-oriented type who is bored by details. In contrast to the sensation type, intuitives are mainly interested in seeing the possibilities beyond what is present or obvious or known about the situation. An emphasis on possibilities will usually get through to an intuitive.

MANAGEMENT AUDIENCES

For the most part, management audiences are sensation/thinker types. These people hate an intuitive's perceptive, wandering discussion. For those types, the intuitive speaker has to do two things: listen to them and then close in and tell them something, and this something has to be logical and structured. Sensation/thinker audiences don't like unstructured ideas; they want solutions to specific problems. Intuitives among the audience, however, want to hear about the possibilities, and feeling types want to feel a relationship before they will really tune in. Therefore, the individual addressing an audience has to review the speech in all these terms, and touch base with all these needs. (Figure 4.1.)

To have validity also, the speech has to touch base with memory and belief so that the facts the speaker uses are consistent with the memories and beliefs of the listeners and their understanding of the facts. You have to penetrate all the rings of type to reach the memory and belief, and then the unconscious in the inner circle. While executives are accustomed to having their speeches written for them, they must be aware of the fact that their primary task is to communicate with the audience

Figure 4.1. Anatomy of a speech.

rather than to recite dry information. The fact that most executive speeches are written with the idea that they will eventually appear in print compounds the communications problem.

Thus, a speech also takes a little sensitivity. Architects, for example, who are accustomed to selling ideas verbally to potential or actual clients, are often extroverted; that is, they are in touch with the subject, in this case the client. They will frequently use sketches to illustrate concepts before nonprofessionals because these communicate creative ideas to thinker/sensation types who need concreteness. Thus, the architect, a more developed aesthetic than his or her audience, is able to influence and shape the undeveloped, undifferentiated aesthetics of the client by picking up on the client's type function, although he or she is usually unconscious of the process.

An intuitive client, on the other hand, will be captured by the possibilities and can see the possibilities, so the architect can create another kind of presentation what will touch this person.

Typing of communicating styles teaches us to recognize audiences, whether group or individual, and reach them through the functions.

Awareness of the feelings that are being expressed can come from any or all of the senses: all cues are not verbal. Body posture and facial expression are two nonverbal cues. A strong verbal cue can come from the use of metaphor. Football expressions and word pictures are often used to express feelings inadvertently:

"He should have made an end run but he dropped the ball."

"She sailed right past me."

"Run it up the flagpole and see if anybody salutes."

There is, in bad communication, also an absence of feeling. According to C. Northcote Parkinson:

A declining institution, whether a country, a university, a trade union, or a business enterprise, is one in which the leaders have lost their way, have forgotten above all what exactly they are trying to do. The creation of the vacuum is due to basic causes that need, for their proper analysis, not a page but a book. If the causes are obscure and complex, however, the symptoms are obvious and one of them is the failure to communicate.[2]

Such failure or loss of vision is really a failure of feeling because feeling is the function that expresses values.

These are all examples of indirect communication of feeling: disappointment, chagrin, hope. Some people cloak really violent emotion in cursing, or else they cover up fear in verbal contempt. These are pretty extreme, but they are safety valves when people do not want to confront feelings directly. Psychologists offer various tactics for dealing with the negative emotions of others in a situation like negotiation or business discussion where an outburst of temper could be fatal or where humiliation is being used as a technique. These tactics include impassivity, reasonableness, and silence, but the refusal to be humiliated or intimidated is used most often. People begin with the recognition that their feelings are being attacked rather than denying or repressing this knowledge.

Another problem with feelings and words is simple misunderstanding. We are not sensitive or familiar enough with others to know the context in which they use words. Thus, in negotiation, what appears to be a refusal to negotiate may only be the opening move. "That's unacceptable," can mean "the meeting is over," or "what else have you to offer?" The skilled negotiator feels the atmosphere out and interprets it correctly. Feeling can be evoked destructively when, for example, a bullying or harassing manner is employed under the delusion that it projects strength, a danger we now face in diplomatic negotiations. In our society, an overbearing, angry, or stern manner can simply isolate the person

[2]Ibid.

using it from others who are more skilled at interpersonal relationships. Often, the "bully" is projecting an outmoded, authoritarian style and does not understand the rejection he or she gets. This person is "out of touch with his or her feelings" and the feelings of others. This kind of problem is not really one of feelings but of style.

Body language is an important way of communicating. Nonverbal communication includes tone of voice, pacing, sounds, facial expressions, and body posture. This kind of message can be safer and truer because it is not precise. Clearly, there is no single meaning to a gesture. For example, it is thought that arms folded across the chest is supposed to mean that the person's mind is closed to the speaker. But no gesture has a single, unvarying meaning. The meaning of any gesture depends on cultural norms, personal style, the setting, what has gone before, and what both parties anticipate for the future. Because nonverbal behavior is more spontaneous, it is usually a better clue to the individual's real feelings than words. "Some research indicates that facial expression, along with tone of voice, accounts for more than 90% of the communication between two people."[3]

When a person has a vision, communication usually follows from the vision. This is another example of how the functions interact with each other in the workings of the psyche. A clear vision is differentiated feeling. Someone with a vision knows what he or she wants to do. With this knowledge, a way of expressing the feeling or vision can be found because there is something to communicate: something clear and definite.

A good example of a company with a vision is Tandem

[3]Michael B. McCaskey, "The Hidden Messages Managers Send," *Harvard Business Review*, November–December, 1979.

Computers and its CEO, Jim Treybig. Treybig has reduced his vision to five cardinal points of running a company: (1) all people are good; (2) people, workers, management, and company are all the same thing; (3) every single person in a company must understand the essence of the business; (4) every employee must benefit from the company's success; and (5) one must create an environment where all of the above can happen. Many consider that his management theory, which includes rhetoric about how the company represents "the convergence of capitalism and humanism" is heavy slugging, but all agree that the message has been fully communicated. There is a spirit in Tandem that expresses the clarity of the founder's vision.[4]

TYPE AND SALES EFFECTIVENESS: COMMUNICATING WITH PROSPECTIVE CUSTOMERS

One of the leading sales trainers in the world, John Molloy, has conducted an extensive study of sales effectiveness.[5] His research has led to a number of important insights about what makes a person an effective salesperson. These are:

1.   If you look at any sales force, you will find that 20 percent of the people do 80 percent of the work. Twenty percent are real salespeople and the rest are ordertakers. Oddly enough, nothing changes if you give the salesforce sales training. The reason is that sales training by

[4]"Managing by Mystique at Tandem Computers," *Fortune*, June 28, 1982, pp. 84–87.
[5]John T. Molloy, *Molloy's Live for Success*, New York: William Morrow, 1981.

and large does not work. Sales training fails because sales trainers believe there is only one way to sell. The fact is that there is not a single way to sell. Selling must involve the total personality of the prospect. For example, a sure way to failure is for a woman to sell like a man. This never works. Male sales trainers will tell you to keep good eye contact with your prospect or you will turn buyers off. Women know that if you keep good eye contact with your prospect you will turn buyers on. Women know that if they smile too much, no one will take them seriously, and the first task of a woman in a sales situation is to be taken seriously. Molloy's rule: never smile for at least the first 10 minutes of the first meeting, until you establish the fact that you are a serious businessperson.

2.   There are two psychological principles that great salespeople use: First is the *yes* principle. Get the prospect in the habit of saying yes. "Do you want your wife and children to enjoy the same standard of living that you now have after you are gone?" "Isn't it a beautiful day!" This principle is based on the fact that thinking and action are, in part, matters of habit and, if you can get people into a positive frame of mind, your chances of getting a sale are greater.

3.   Join the opposition. Great salespeople never argue. No matter what the prospect says, agree. This may sound like lying, but in fact it is based on a sound psychological principle. Rapport is based on communication, and communication is an interaction between a message sender and a message receiver. If a prospect says, "I hate green," these words are an effort to communicate a message. The message is more likely to be picked up if you agree with the statement than if you disagree. If a prospect says that the product is too expensive, the great salesperson says, "Yes, but, it has this and that feature, and it is really worth the money." What

is going on here is the building of rapport, which is a fancy way of saying the building up of a feeling connection. The good salesperson recognizes the reality of feeling and instinctively knows that, in order to sell, there must be a good rapport, that rapport comes with communication, and that communication is sending and receiving messages. If you are a salesperson, part of your job is to receive messages. The other part of your job is to send messages.

4. Sending messages is a matter of reading your prospect. This must be done on many levels. One level is reading your prospect's type. Is the prospect an ST (sensation/thinking type) or an NF (intuition/feeling type)? These are both perceptive types who will be sold by the facts in the case of the ST or by the possibilities in the case of the NF. Is your prospect a TS (thinking/sensation type) or an FN (feeling/intuition type)? These are both judging types who will be influenced by a logical presentation, in the case of the TS, or by a sensitivity to their values, in the case of the FN.

5. One of the key qualities of effective salespeople is that they are calmer than poor salespeople. Good salespeople have smooth and unhurried movements. They make no jerky motions. They do not surprise. They never pull a rabbit out of a hat. Poor salespeople are what Molloy called "jumpies." They are nervous. They move too quickly. They give the impression of being upset, and they communicate this to the buyer.

6. Good salespeople have a good sixth sense, or intuition. They know when they are crowding a prospect and back off. They do not come physically close to clients until they can do this without offending. Bad salespeople do just the opposite; they invade others' territory, they don't listen, and they turn people off completely.

7. This intuition can be developed through training. The simplest is one-on-one critique of sales ap-

proaches. An instructor or friend can tell you when you are giving positive verbal and nonverbal messages. Getting this feedback can provide a check on your intuition. Comparing your intuitive perception with the actual report of the "reactor" will, over time, develop your intuitive power.

ST = sensation/thinking	TS = thinking/sensation
NF = intuition/feeling	FN = feeling/intuition

8.   One of the most effective sales boosting techniques is the motivational meeting. A person who sells 1,000 widgets will sell 1,100 if he or she is highly motivated. Motivation creates enthusiasm, and enthusiasm sells. This is a technique that focuses on feeling.

9.   A second sale boosting technique is product knowledge—up to a point. The best product knowledge position is to know a little more than your client. Knowing a lot more may kill the sale. The reason for this is simple: if you know a little more, you will be much better able to communicate with your client because you will know where she or he is. If you know a lot more, chances are you will have forgotten where your client is, and you will not be able to communicate well. You will expound your knowledge beyond your client's understanding and lose contact with your client.

10.   Client analysis is one of the areas that can have the greatest impact in training salespeople. The essence of client analysis is teaching people to use varied approaches, depending on whom they are dealing with. One of the ways of analyzing clients is to estimate their typology. If you are not certain of their type preference, then you should make sure that your appeals relate to

both functions of perception *and* both functions of judgment. By doing this, you are ensuring that regardless of your client's type, one part of your appeal will be directed to the client's type preference.

Conclusion

The secret to an effective communicating style is to tune in on your target audience's wave length. If the target is a person, your challenge is to estimate the type preference of the individual and communicate or send messages on the target's type of wave length. If you are communicating with a group, the task is more complicated because you are very likely to have each of the types in an audience of any size. To communicate effectively, you should make sure that your message has, in effect, something for everybody, or, more precisely, something for each of the types in the audience. The sensates will appreciate a practical, factual, here-and-now approach. The feeling types will appreciate a good rapport with the authorities. The thinking types will appreciate a logical and well-organized presentation, and the intuitives will enjoy hearing about the possibilities that are associated with your subject.

5

Type and Time: What Are You Doing for Me Yesterday, Today, and Tomorrow?

Those who make the worst use of their time most complain of its shortness.

LA BRUYERE

One of the most demanding tasks of management is relating the objectives and programs of the organization to time. It is commonplace to recognize the uncertainty that surrounds the future, but the fact is that there is also tremendous uncertainty surrounding the past. As a senior executive once put it, "In this organization, the past is more uncertain than the future." What he meant was that the "memory" of the past was selective, and the version of the past that was accepted was a function as much of the people who were in power as it was of the objective facts.

One of the principal skills of management is deciding what to do today and what to do tomorrow. The ability of management to manage the tradeoff between the short- and long-run is critical to the success of the enterprise. With too much emphasis on the short-run present, the company is in danger of falling behind the competition in product development and innovation, which require investment in the present for future payoff. If there is too much emphasis on the long-run future, the company runs the danger of not meeting the competition's value offering to the customer in the current market. If the past is not adequately understood, then the basis for present action will be based on incorrect assumptions about the nature of reality.

What should be done today; what should be done tomorrow; and what is the significance of the past? These are the temporal questions that every manager faces in the job every day. It is widely agreed that one of the ways in which American managers have slipped in their performance, vis-à-vis managers in other countries, is the emphasis in the United States on the short-run, quarter-to-quarter bottom line. This is in contrast to the approach in Japan, for example, where managers often look to a lifetime instead of the quarter as a planning horizon. For instance, Mr. Koichi Tsukamoto, President of Wacoal Corporation, commented in a recent interview, "In January of 1950, when I was approaching my thirtieth year, I felt it was a good time to make a fifty-year-plan, which would carry us through to the end of the century and my eightieth birthday, should I live."[1]

One of the more fascinating aspects of psychological

---

[1]"Working a Miracle through Mutual Trust—Interview with Mr. Koichi Tsukamoto, President of Wacoal Corp., *PHP*, October 1981, p. 69.

types is the difference in basic temporal orientation of different types. Mann, Siegler, & Osmond, in a landmark study,[2] observed that there are in people four basic time orientations, and that these orientations are linked to the primary or leading function.

> At first we observed that thinking types related to time in a linear fashion; that is, things were experienced in terms of the process of relating past to present to future, in what we have termed the time line. The three other possibilities involve a more exclusive concentration on one of these particular dimensions; that is, either predominant relationship to the past, or to the present, or to the future. We have observed that feeling types relate primarily to the past, sensation types to the present and intuitives to the future.[3]

The time orientation of the functions is described in the remainder of this chapter.

SENSATION: THE PRESENT

Sensation is the function that perceives the immediate situation. Sensates surpass all others in the ability to perceive the present moment. They respond without hesitation to environmental stimuli, and their response is to the stimulus presented by the object itself, not a prearranged plan or commitment.

The sensation type is a realist who accepts and operates on the basis of facts, whatever these may be. They

[2]Harriet Mann, Miriam Siegler, and Humphrey Osmond, "The Many Worlds of Time," *Journal of Analytical Psychology*, 13, pp. 33–56. The descriptions which follow draw heavily on this classic work.
[3]Ibid., p. 36.

know exactly what is going on. More than any other type, they have an acute sense of the present reality of any situation. They love facts and can remember and use them well.

The time orientation of sensation types accounts for their efficiency and superior ability in dealing with crises and emergencies of any kind. They are the proverbial troubleshooters, the type who can come in and "clean up" a mess. They do not agonize over alternative courses of action; the event itself tells them what to do. Because they are so geared to the present, sensates see much more in a situation than any other type. Their ability to read the depth of the present is their way of substituting or compensating for their lack of futurity or their memory of the past. Since much of life does not lend itself to planning, many things are best dealt with by direct response when a new stimulus presents itself. In these situations, the sensation type is at a distinct advantage.

FEELING: THE PAST

For the feeling type, time is circular. The past lives in the present and immediately returns to the past as a memory. Feeling types are collectors of memories. They tend to see present situations in terms of what is similar to the past, rather than in terms of what is unique. Feeling types have difficulty in being punctual since the on-going emotion of whatever they are involved in is more demanding than mere commitments or clocks. They are likely to remain too long at a meeting or meal, and extend a brief chat into a long conversation. When a thinking type and a feeling type are together, the thinking type will often feel that time is dragging as the conversation goes on and on. It is hard for the feeling type to disengage from an interaction, even if failing to disengage will cause problems for them in other areas of their lives.

Feeling types tend to relate the present to the past, so that time past becomes time present. There is obviously great value in this time orientation. The future is to come, and the present is only this precise moment. Most of what we know in life comes from past experience.

Since people of different types experience the world very differently, at least some of those conflicts that occur between spouses, parents and children, scientific adversaries, political figures, and business associates need no longer be ascribed to sociocultural differences, "bad faith," or even neurosis. While common sense and conventional wisdom tell us that we all see the same event, type theory suggests that conflicts occur because the "same" event, occurring at the same time for different people, is, in fact, a different event for each of them.

THE FORD MOTOR COMPANY EDSEL PROJECT: LOOKING BACKWARD

Of all American business failures, none has been more examined, studied, or hashed over than that of the Ford Motor Company's disastrous introduction of the Edsel in 1957. The design and marketing of the Edsel were preceded by the most extensive research operation ever documented for a consumer product: a six-volume study based on the concept of "environmental assessment," or study of the "threats and opportunities" of the environment to a company's resources. The study was commissioned in 1948 by Henry Ford II, who was concerned that people who bought Fords when they were young were moving to General Motors' middle-range cars when they became more affluent, rather than to Ford's middle-priced Mercury.

Based on this study, which was basically a forecast of U.S. economic conditions in 1965, Ford went ahead with the Edsel and released it in 1957. It survived until the 1960 model year, costing the Ford Motor Company around $350 million in the process. The introduction of the Edsel was preceded by mammoth market research, by huge advertising outlays, and by all the resources of the country's second largest automobile company. What went wrong? One way of explaining this failure is in terms of thinking, feeling, sensation, and intuition and how they were misapplied to the problem.

The study and the program were turned over to a group within Ford called the Forward Product Planning Committee, under the direction of Richard Krafve, the division's assistant general manager. The six-volume report that he had caused to be prepared for the Committee projected an increase of $135 billion in gross national product for the coming 10-year period, with an increase of twenty million new cars for a total of 70 million cars in operation. More than 50 percent of American families would enjoy incomes of over $5,000 per year, the threshold for upward mobility to a medium-priced car. Thus, more than 10 percent of all cars sold would be in the medium- to high-priced category. The study recommended that Ford tap this new market with a new car that would not just be a new model but a new make.

It is obvious that Krafve and his group expected that the already-perceived trend in the 1950s toward medium-priced over lower-priced cars would continue. Even low-priced cars were being sold loaded with accessories. The more expensive cars in the lower price ranges were selling better than the lower-priced cars. Those people who did buy lower-priced cars when they were younger were now trading up as their incomes increased. Krafve and his group went with this line. They did not, for example, examine all the possibilities and then draw on the most probable. Their proposition was that the market for cars was solely income-determined and that higher incomes would result in the medium-priced cars selling. Mercury, however, was not doing well. Therefore, the conclusion was that to remain in business Ford had to introduce a new, medium-priced brand.

In April 1955, the proposal of the Forward Product Planning Committee was approved, and a new group, the Special Products Division, was created and headed by Krafve. David Wallace was hired as director of planning for market research. He was to name the new "E-car" ("E" for experimental) and develop a marketing image for it. Both men were primarily "introverted thinkers," and it was this typology that determined the outcome of the Edsel project. Introverts are slow to respond to external stimuli, are unspontaneous, and are defensive against the "object." Thinkers are able organizers and administrators, are preoccupied with the flow of time from past through the present to the future, with emphasis on preserving the continuity of the process. They are methodical and logical but also unspontaneous and lacking in the intuitive's leap of understanding. They are often plodders, looking straight ahead (or behind), but ignoring any kind of peripheral action, often defending against facts that do not agree with their thesis. They tend to develop a theory and then relate the situation to it.

Krafve was totally convinced that the thrust of his report was the only possible outcome, that the trends perceived would continue through the 1950s and 1960s. He applied the same detailed, logical approach to the problem of design. "Krafve was not the kind of man to envision his objective in a single, revelatory flash; instead he anatomized the styling of the E-car into a series of laboriously minute decisions. . . . later calculated to involve at least four thousand separate styling decisions."[4]

The Edsel was to be launched in September 1957. In July 1957, the stock market dropped in the beginning of the recession of 1958. In early August, medium-priced 1957 cars declined in sales, and the situation ended with dealers of all makes ending their season with the second-largest number of unsold new cars in history. Sales of the Rambler, however, the only American-made small car available, rose sharply. Why, you might ask, did Krafve fail to react to this? One factor was typology. Thinking types ignore facts that do not bear out their theories. As a thinking type, Krafve was also guided by his sense of continuity. As he explained to Brooks, he could not drop the program because dealers had been signed up, the contracts had to be honored, and the new car produced. As has been pointed out, thinkers make excellent scientists because of their ability to apply logic, their sense of a linear time frame from past through the present to the future, and their discipline. Unfortunately, if they are working with a wrong premise, those same admirable traits can lead them down the garden path to disaster. David Wallace, the Special Products Division director of planning for market research, was also an introverted thinker. He and Krafve had both decided that the Edsel's image should be completely different. This image was derived from extensive market testing of the advanced models, the first such procedure under-

---

[4]John Brooks, *Business Adventures*, (New York: Weybright and Talley, 1969).

taken in the industry. Wallace, a creative thinker, believed that cars represented wish fulfillment to American males. People bought cars because of their image, not because of practical features. A basic element of the image is the car's name. Several research firms were retained to do market studies in New York, Chicago, and Ann Arbor, with the objective of finding the right name. Two thousand possible choices were tested. The poet Marianne Moore was retained. An advertising agency was retained whose solution was a contest among its international offices. An additional 6,000 names were generated by a computer program. Market research indicated that Krafve's original suggestion, Edsel, was unfavorable; Krafve was not deterred and Edsel prevailed. As a thinking type, Krafve was not swayed by information unfavorable to his thesis.

A publicity man, C. Gayle Warnock, who was an extroverted sensation type, was hired. Sensation types need immediate feedback; they cannot visualize future rewards. Their response to stimuli is direct and immediate, unlike the slow reaction of the thinker. Krafve wanted Warnock to "program" the publicity; that is, to work back from Introduction Day and schedule the efforts. Warnock was used to working from day to day, taking the breaks when he could get them. As a sensation type, Warnock had a better grasp of the immediate situation. He realized that the elaborate secrecy with which the publicity had been orchestrated up to his arrival on the scene might build up expectations that no car, short of a rocket ship, could satisfy. He expressed these doubts to Krafve. But thinkers are suspicious of sensation types because they move so fast and are so present-oriented that they do not consider alternative courses of action. The two men finally agreed on a strategy that was a compromise; individual features of the car would be revealed, little by little, but the car would not be totally unveiled until its introduction. Finally, a three-day press junket was arranged, involving travel and accommodations for 250 reporters and their wives from all over the country, an affair that cost Ford over $90,000.

Based on his need for quick sensation-type results, Warnock made a number of decisions. Enjoined by Krafve from publicizing speed and horsepower, he decided to dramatize it by staging a hair-raising test by stunt drivers. One of the cars nearly flipped. He arranged a fashion show for the reporters' wives, at which the "couturier" turned out to be a female impersonator. He employed the Ray McKinley band for the evening gala and, not having an active memory, forgot that the band had been formed by Glenn Miller, so the dancing reporters were faced with large "GMs" on every band stand.

The next morning, true to his type, Warnock offered 70 cars to reporters to drive home without waiting to make sure they were bug free. The objective of this drive-away program was to receive favorable publicity from reporters who had first-hand driving experience. Unfortunately, the cars lost oil pans; motors froze; brakes failed; and there were two collisions—one caused by a rubbernecking driver on the Pennsylvania Turnpike who wanted a better look at the strange new car.

Finally, a feeling type entered the scene in the person of J. C. Doyle, general sales and marketing manager of the Special Products Division. Directed by Krafve to set up a new distribution network instead of using the one already in place, Doyle approached it with his extroverted feeling characteristics. In a time sense, feeling types see the present as a consequence of the past. They do not see the new as unique but as a spin-off from something already experienced. Thus, Doyle objected to

Wallace's efforts to personalize the Edsel. Doyle went along, but his need, as a feeling type, to maintain relationships on a personal basis made him suffer more than the others. He felt, in the end, that the company had given the public what it wanted, but the public had turned on the company. Instead, the fickle public chose the little beetles.

Typologically, what went wrong? The development team had each function available to them—thinking, sensation, and feeling—except one, intuition. Intuition might have helped them realize that the American consumer was shifting from income-related buying to taste-related buying. All of the information was there; the cultural explosion of the 1960s had already begun. More Americans than ever before were traveling, and travel, education, and culture were becoming the new status symbols rather than items of conspicuous consumption such as new cars. Intuition is the function that relates to the future. Yet, Wallace and Krafve, both primarily thinkers, were unable to free themselves from the logical progress of past–present–future to make that intuitive leap that would have informed them of the possibilities— one of the possibilities being that their research conclusions were wrong.

They were also insensitive to the public reaction against Detroit-made cars. One indicator of a change in public taste was the young men who were "customizing" their chrome-laden Detroit cars by taking off frills, wheel covers, and other options, and cutting down the ubiquitous, "sexy" fins. The flashy Edsel went completely against this trend.

The Edsel is a lesson in the folly of past-based research when times are changing. Never in the history of world business was more money spent on marketing research. And never has there been a more spectacular failure of a new product than the Edsel. The missing element in the Edsel project was intuition, perception of the possibilities. Lacking intuition, all associated with the project were literally flying blind.

INTUITION: THE FUTURE

Intuition is the function that relates primarily to the future and is the least understood of the alternative experiential worlds. Intuition, the function that tries to ascertain that which is possible, is discontinuous in the same way that sensation is discontinuous. Sensation fails to integrate the past into the present and the present into the future. Intuition fails to integrate past and present into the future. For the intuitive, the present is a pale shadow, the past is a mist; excitement, warmth, and sunshine are to be found beyond the next bend in the road, or on the other side of the mountain. Intuitives spend their lives in a race toward the next beyond. They are like a person trying to capture a hat blown by the wind; as he or she gets closer, another gust catches it and drives it farther on. For this person, the future continually recedes.[5]

Because intuitives are constantly generating new visions of future possibilities, they tend to skip about rapidly from one activity to another. As soon as a new inspiration presents itself, their curiosity is piqued and they want to see how it will turn out. While others are trying to catch up with the vision of the intuitive, the intuitive is more than likely to have abandoned the vision to follow some new inspiration. For this reason, intuitives often fail to benefit from their inspirations.

[5]Mann, Siegler, and Osmond, Op. Cit., p. 50.

Others pursue and develop the visions intuitives initiate and reap the fruit of the seeds sown by the intuitive. Thus, unless an intuitive develops his or her own auxiliary functions, or pairs with a thinking or feeling type, he or she is like a ship without a rudder. It can keep going, but there is no assurance that it will arrive at the appointed place.[6]

Because they are speedy and cannot resist anticipating new possibilities, intuitives frequently fail to master the necessary skills of any activity. This speed factor accounts for the love of excitement and chaos that is notable in many intuitives, particularly in extroverted intuitives. Introverted intuitives really want more than anything else to be left alone, to follow their visions without interference from the so-called real world. Interference discourages them. Their faith and intuition make them independent and individualistic, and certainly the least prone of any of the types to conform.

Intuitives appear to others to be impractical and unrealistic. But if we accept four realities: (1) the thinking reality of process and ideas, (2) the feeling reality of memory, (3) the sensation reality of immediate concreteness, and (4) the intuitive reality of anticipation and possibility, we can see that intuitives are as practical and as realistic as other types in their own special mode of perception.

THINKING: THE LINE OF TIME

Thinking is a rational, continuous function that relates to time as a line. Time, for the thinking type, is a flowing from the past through the present and into the future.

---

[6]Ibid., p. 52.

The concern with time's flow creates a primary characteristic of the thinking type in relation to time, that is, the predominance of the process over any element or combination of elements that comprise a situation. Because thinkers are concerned with process rather than with the episode, planning is an important aspect of the way they relate to life. Thinking types are the great planners of the world. No other type can equal them in their ability to plot things through time. Unfortunately, thinking types take plans so seriously that they often ignore General Patton's maxim: "One does not plan and then try to make circumstances fit the plans. One tries to make plans fit the circumstances." The great danger in the thinking type is a tendency toward rigidity. Such individuals often become disoriented and confused when required to deviate from the plan.

While the definitive assessment of the personality of Richard Nixon has yet to be written, he has fascinated many writers. This book is not the place to put forth the various psychological theories about him and refute or defend them, but there is an interesting conjecture to be had in the Nixon experience in terms of typology—particularly in relation to the typologically oriented sense of time. Nixon behaved as an "introverted thinking type." He was able to view time as a continuum stretching from the past through the present to the future and thus manage Ehrlichman and Haldeman, two extroverted sensation types, who were able to "seize the moment" but rarely looked forward or back. Nixon's sense of history and his determination to be viewed by posterity as a great president are seen as the reasons for his fatal attempts to control the press and his inability to destroy the tapes that would "reveal" him to future generations.

Case Example: Admiral Hyman Rickover

Admiral Hyman Rickover is one of America's great military leaders. Often described as the father of the nuclear Navy, Admiral Rickover has an extraordinary capacity to get his way in Washington. Presidents come and go, but for four decades Rickover has been a permanent fixture on the Washington scene. Typologically, Rickover is an introverted thinking intuitive. As an intuitive, he has a capacity for seeing into the future, and as a thinker he has the capacity for seeing the line of time that turns an idea or plan into reality. The motto on the wall of his office is from the *Book of Proverbs*: "Where there is no vision the people perish."

In addition to being an introverted thinking intuitive, Rickover is a forceful personality, and he is also a person with relatively undifferentiated feeling. He has the visionary's capacity to persist in the face of indifference and disapproval. For the intuitive, facts don't matter. What matters is the idea, and since the idea comes from within rather than without, there is constant energy to guide and fuel effort.

According to his staff, Rickover hypothesizes a truth and then selects the "facts" to prove his hypothesis. He suppresses any facts that do not support his position. This often looks like a heresy to his extroverted staffers, but to Rickover, the facts do not matter. They are relevant only if they support the idea, the vision, of what the future should be.

Rickover's intuitiveness, his indifference to the feelings of others, and his willingness to use fear as a goad to obtain his ends are all part of the ruthless (as seen especially by extroverts) qualities that often go with the strong and forceful introverted personality. He likes displays of power and pomp (unconscious sensation?), and yet he cloaks himself in a Spartan image and holds his staff to Spartan discipline, obedience, and commitment to his goal of establishing a nuclear Navy. As a thinking intuitive, Rickover lives on the line of time with a special emphasis and strength of vision for the future. He collects raw data, analyzes them, and reaches a conclusion. Instead of calling his conclusion a prediction, he calls it a project and makes it happen. He creates the future by dedication to his vision of what the future should look like. His methods are often harsh and even cruel because he is insensitive and indifferent to the feelings of people. This side of his personal style reflects his unconscious feeling and sensation. In the place of empathy and understanding, he relies on fear, intimidation, and the threat of public humiliation. These are not recommended methods for motivating people, but they do, in fact, work for Admiral Rickover. He forges a management style that expresses his personality and achieves his vision.

6

Creating a Balance: Type and the Management Team

God has put as differing talents in man as trees in Nature; and each talent, like each tree, has its own special character and aspect. The finest pear tree in the world cannot produce the most ordinary apple, the most splendid talent cannot duplicate the effect of the homeliest skill.

LA ROCHEFOUCAULD[1]

INTRODUCTION

An individual's typology has profound implications for the way he or she adapts to life, and in particular, for the roles he or she plays in work. One of the joys in life is observing a person in a job or profession to which she or he is truly suited. Even the Preacher in Ecclesiastes,

[1]From the maxims of La Rochefoucauld, translated by Louis Kronenberger, Random House, Inc. New York, 1959, p. 128.

after his lament "all is vanity," says "there is nothing better for a man [or a woman] than that he [or she] should eat and drink and find enjoyment in his [or her] toil."

Typological preferences define not only what we enjoy and are comfortable doing but also what we do best. For example:

Sensation types can do a superb job of managing factual details and supervision where accuracy is important.

Intuitive people are best at dealing with the big picture and holistic perception of possibilities.

Thinkers excel at impersonal, logical, systematic sorting out of perceptions of actuality and possibilities in a situation.

Strength, for a feeling type, is the ability to experience a broader range of feelings directly.

Face-to-face dealings with people require extroversion.

Solitude and concentration require introversion.

What is the best type for management? What is the best combination of types for an organization? Should an organization seek people of similar types, or should it seek diversity? Is there any relationship between type effectiveness and the requirements of managing businesses at different stages of the life cycle? These questions are addressed in this chapter.

BIRDS OF A FEATHER

People, like birds, tend to flock together based on type similarity. The reason for this is simple. People of the same type adapt to life in the same way. There is an easy familiarity in being with a person of the same type. You see the world in the same way, and as a consequence, feel comfortable. Unfortunately, feeling comfortable is not really the best basis for choosing members of a management team.

Recall for example, the case described in the introduction. The founder and president of a company that developed a new packaging technique was an introverted intuitive. He saw early on the possibilities in this technique and very creatively exploited these possibilities. By doing so, he established his company as a leader in the field. As the industry matured, however, the critical success requirements shifted from creative product development to cost management. But the president himself remained the same man, with the same one-sided interest in creativity and the development of new ideas. What did he do? He brought in a bright young M.B.A. who was a "bird of a feather," in other words, his own type. The two of them continued to generate new ideas and blue-sky opportunities when what was needed was another kind of person who could come into that business, manage costs, and turn it into a low-cost, high-volume, efficient competitor. The company diversified into new and "exciting" ventures instead of concentrating on the boring job of managing costs. While the company moved into exciting areas, the basic business began to decline in profitability and competitive position.

There is a different typological phenomenon in interpersonal relationships: the complementarity of opposites. Typically (but not always), a combination will include a husband who is the thinker and a wife who is the feeler. The man's feeling function is largely unconscious (inferior). This creates a situation in which there is a sense of something missing in the man's conscious mind. This man will then typically look for and find a woman who has differentiated feeling and largely un-conscious thinking. The two marry and experience bliss—at first—because in this single act of coming to-gether each has filled a great void. But as the couple matures, each may decide to develop within him- or her-self the function of the mate. The effort may bring them closer or to the divorce courts, ending the fusion that brought them together in the first place.

Frequently, in marriage, conflict is based on typolog-ical grounds. But if the couple can work through differ-ences in the way they perceive each other's typologies and the world, the effort itself can solidify the marriage.

While love and marriage relationships are usually based on type complementarity—the attraction of op-posites—in business as well as in friendships, the at-traction is usually to type similarity. People of the same type see and relate to the world in the same way and are, therefore, comfortable with each other. This tendency is often the basis for a common mistake in creating man-agement groups: picking birds of a feather instead of complementary types for members of the team.

GE TESTS THE BIRDS-OF-A-FEATHER SYNDROME

At General Electric, I participated in an investigation conducted by Kenneth O. Michel (now a vice-president at GTE) concerning how individuals process informa-tion to arrive at decisions or shape their perceptions. Michel's group was interested in the research that had been done on the left brain—right brain phenomenon. The primary purpose of the study was to improve the presentation of information to individuals so that each would process it in a way that would be compatible with his or her individual left or right brain orientation. The

Jungian typology theory, in Michel's view, supports the left brain–right brain findings. GE started by testing a group of 112 senior functional managers from a diversity of businesses in GE with the Myers-Briggs Type Indicator Test. (Later, as a business-oriented refinement, Michel used the Keegan Type Indicator to reinforce the Myers-Briggs findings.) This was done during three consecutive courses given to the group. The test results were scored by an independent consulting firm. Michel and I then devised an experiment, based on one reported on by Mitroff and Kilman in *Management Review*.

One of the most interesting experiments ever conducted toward finding an approach to organizational problem solving was the use and analysis of "Stories Managers Tell," by Ian I. Mitroff and Ralph H. Kilman,[2] two University of Pittsburgh Graduate School professors. They have found that similar psychological types emerge with the same "organizational myths" if they are allowed to develop stories that represent their idea of the ideal organization without ridicule or criticism. They have determined, for example, that ST (sensing/feeling) types emphasize day-to-day specifics with emphasis on detail; NT (intuition/feeling) types concentrate on long-range human goals; and SF (sensing/feeling) types view day-to-day human relationships. Thus, "all problems of any importance not only have features that involve every one of these aspects but organizational problems ought to be conceptualized as such," they say. "We would argue that the failure to view problems as involving all four viewpoints can be disastrous to an organization. By ignoring one or more of these viewpoints, an organiza-

[2]Ian I. Mitroff and Ralph H. Kilman, "Stories Managers Tell," *Management Review*, July 1975, pp. 18–27.

tion can fail to recognize and hence to treat an important side of its problems."[3]

Like the Mitroff–Kilman study, we asked each of the participants to describe an ideal organization. There were no specifications placed on the type of organization. Each gave her or his description and, on the basis of the description, was assigned to a team.

It is interesting to note that, out of the 112 participants, all senior managers, ten (or 8 percent) were tested as sensers; ten (or 8 percent) as intuitives; 92 (or 75 percent) as thinkers, and twelve (or 10 percent) as feelers. Spouses of this group who were also tested came out this way: 23 (or 26 percent) were sensers; four (or 17 percent) were intuitives; four (or 17 percent) were thinkers, and nine (or 39 percent) were feelers. There was complementarity between wives and husbands, with a typical combination being a thinker husband and a feeler wife.

Each of the manager teams was asked to come to a consensus on a description of the ideal organization and prepare a five-minute flip chart presentation of its conclusion. Unknown to the participants, each had been assigned to a team on the basis of individual Jungian typology characteristics as revealed by the tests. The results were dramatic. Everyone on the team expressed opinions on the basis of typology, and in consensus with everybody else on the team.

Those in the team of thinkers and sensers explained the ideal organizational chart structure, with boxes and lines describing positions and relationships. The intuitive-feelers described the organization in words and phrases, predominantly explaining people relationships. The team whose dominant typology was sensation oriented

[3]Ibid., p. 26.

explained the organization in task-oriented descriptions and hierarchical diagrams. The teams with dominant intuitive typology described the organization in broader terminology, such as "marketing" or "technology" or "finance." The typology categorization was overwhelmingly predictive of the characteristics of the responses, in Michel's view and mine.

THE UNBALANCED ORGANIZATION

Similarly, in the real situation of business, executives often tend to "flock" according to their typology. This tendency can create tunnel vision at the top that can seriously warp the management resources of a company.

One of the dangers of insufficient awareness of one's own psychological type is precisely this tendency: to associate with types similar to our own almost exclusively. Because people of the same type perceive and decide on the same basis as we do, they are easy to understand and comfortable to be with. Other types may be disturbing or seem abrasive. The problem arises when, by associating almost exclusively with our own type, we cut ourselves off from complementary types who can reinforce our strengths and compensate for our weaknesses. As we have seen with the birds-of-a-feather case study, in the case of a top manager who is looking for same-type associates to help her or him plan direction and implement the plan, this exclusiveness can be dangerous.

There is also the human tendency to value our own superior function and attitude over those of others. Thus, intuitives often find sensation types boring and unimaginative, and sensation types can find intuitives flighty and out of touch with reality. Thinkers often find feelers nonobjective and unprincipled, and feelers often "feel" thinkers are impersonal and calculating. Extroverts find introverts distant, detached, and cold, while introverts find extroverts effusive and superficial.

One result of this kind of one-sidedness can be a refusal to look at all the aspects of a situation. James Fallows, the Washington editor of the *Atlantic Monthly*, has commented on what he sees as a dangerous reliance on "the theoretical" thinking of America's defense managers. He decries the continued emphasis on spending more and more for technologically superior weapons. The basic problem, as he sees it, is that the American military establishment is "hooked on the theoretical," and their theories are generally wrong. "Their theory of warfare assumes that a future war will be one of attrition, and they absolutely refuse to acknowledge that one sure lesson of past warfare has always taught that the only lesson is to expect the unexpected." Rather than developing a flexible plan designed to meet the unexpected, they are forcing all weapons to conform to "irrelevant" guidelines, with results seen in the cases of the M-16 infantry rifle and the F-16 fighter planes. They are wrong, says Fallows, in their theories about how people act. They have tried to apply standard industrial management procedures to military personnel, when in fact the task of getting people to fight in combat is unique. As for the role of theory in the conduct of nuclear war, Fallows deplores the depth of our ignorance. Only by doing this can we "avoid being panicked by scenarios with no more foundations in fact than other theologians' fiery visions of hell."[4]

[4]James Fallows, *National Defense* (New York: Random House, 1981).

This is only one example of the one-sided emphasis on thinking that characterizes American organizations of all kinds. When this kind of thing happens, sight is lost of all of the other elements that are required for full understanding and effective action. Rather than reject our opposites, we should try to contact our own third and fourth functions *through* our opposites. This is the only way we can express our own talent and strength, based on our conscious and auxiliary functions, in a full and complete manner.

It takes a special effort for the intuitive, for example, to concentrate on working out the details of an idea rather than pursuing the new and more interesting possibilities that present themselves in the process. For the sensation type, it takes a special effort not only to look at the facts, but also to explore and reflect on the possibilities. Thinkers will always explore the logic and cause and effect of a situation, but must let go of this in order to consciously assess their own feelings and the feelings of others. The thinker must abandon formulas and ideas and really listen to the self and others. The feeler, on the other hand, is in close touch with feelings but must make a special effort to grasp the logical aspects of a situation.

In the organization of a business, when one finds partners who are of the same type, one almost always finds trouble; everybody looks at things the same way. Everybody misses the problems and their solutions because they are all undeveloped in the same way. We have seen how this works in a high technology company where the emphasis is on intuition and sensation and thinking are low. We have seen, in the military example, the danger of pure thinking without intuition to hint of the possibilities, and without feeling to get a sense of how people really behave.

COMPLEMENTARITY OF OPPOSITES

Opposite types complement each other. When two people approach a problem from opposite sides, each sees things that are not visible to the other. Unfortunately, since they do not see things from the same point of view, it is often difficult for complementary types to work well together.

In 1975, Dean A. Holt conducted a seven-day management training workshop at the Psychiatric Institute of Washington, D.C., using the Myers-Briggs Type Indicator. The participants were placed in three groups: one representing largely the introverted, intuitive, feeling, perceptive types; the second made up of extroverted, sensate, thinking, judging types; and the third mixed. While his paper[5] on the entire session is fascinating, one aspect of it relates to this phenomenon of complementarity. The three groups were given a problem—a "Lego Man" doll, made up of blocks of wood. Each of the two homogeneous groups was able to solve the problem in its characteristic ways. The mixed group, which Holt called "conflicted," had trouble. He reports that this group was "taken over" by the extroverted types while the others looked on.

Opposite types complement each other, but if there is total complementarity with no bridges between the functions, the result can be a conflicted situation as we saw in the marital conflict example. When two people approach a problem from opposite sides, each sees things the other does not. Unfortunately, since they do not share the same point of view, there can be conflict. But

---

[5]Dean A. Holt, "Use of the MBTI in Management Training," paper delivered before the National Conference on Applications of the Myers-Briggs Type Indicator, Gainesville, Florida, October 16, 1975.

good teamwork can be accomplished when people differ on only one or two of the type aspects. This much difference is useful, and the aspects they share provide a bridge that aids in understanding and communication across the characteristics they do not share.

When opposite types live or work together, it is enormously helpful if they understand the characteristics of type differences in perceiving and making decisions. Different perceptions of different ways of deciding are much less irritating when people understand the origin of the differences. This promotes the recognition of a complementary type who can help illuminate the nature of reality and the criteria for a decision.

The ability to recognize the value and validity of a different way of perceiving and decision-making in a complementary type is an invaluable attribute for an executive. The individual who can rise above instinctive dislike for another who expresses a different point of view and a different value system, and understand that difference and the reason for it, is at a distinct advantage in a situation in which he or she is expected to make an appropriate decision. This approach can also check the tendency to staff up with type similarities only. And it allows the executive to make use of the valuable complementary mind set of the other, and create a balanced team. (See Table 6.1.)

STAFFING THE TASK FORCE—RELATING TYPE TO TASK

The task force is a management team that has been created for a specific purpose. The idea behind the task force is the recognition that input is needed from all of the functional specializations in a company in order to effectively manage the task.

Table 6.1. Type Complementarity

Intuitive Needs Sensing Type	Sensate Needs Intuitive Type	Feeling Needs Thinker Type	Thinker Needs Feeling Type
To focus on the here and now	To focus on the future	To focus on the link between past, present, and future	To remember the past
To read contracts word for word	To recognize possibilities	To analyze and find logical inconsistencies	To recognize people's feelings
To keep track of important details	To recognize what has been left out of a contract	To weigh evidence	To make value judgments
Getting people to buy what we've got or are selling	To focus on the future	To deduce conclusions from data	To bind people together in cooperative endeavor
	To recognize new, essential elements in a situation	To identify similarities and associations	To make a decision when evidence is not conclusive
	To have what people want or are marketing	To apply concepts, rules, and theories	To focus on the unique and particular aspects of a situation
		To make plans	

The selection of a task force is easy in some ways and difficult in others. It is obvious that certain functions should be represented. Input has to be at a certain level: usually vice-presidential, although, especially in high technology companies, specialists such as scientists and engineers and others who could play an important role in the growth and success of the project will be included. For example, many task teams include a lawyer and a public relations executive.

When you consider all of the different disciplines involved, each with its own stake in the company, it is easy to see how the term "task force" can sometimes be a synonym for "chaos." The secret and the key to a successful task force can lie in an understanding of type. A group made up of typologically aware people can accomplish a lot more a lot faster than a group that struggles within itself for power and domination.

It is important to look below the surface. Very few organizations in the U.S. today screen for type when they hire. At the same time, a lot of falsification goes on; people sense that companies want thinker/sensation types and try to underplay their intuitive/feeling qualities. But if a group leader selects people for their complementarity—and not for replication of his or her own type—a team can be built that will have an extraordinary variety of functions at its command. Since people self-select their careers on the basis of type, unless type falsification is involved, if different disciplines are included in a task force it is certain that different types will be also. In particular, the leader must be aware of the typological make-up of the members of the group in order to evaluate, mediate, and draw out the best in the people that are involved. (See Table 6.2.)

This self-selection is usually governed by an inner wisdom. Type studies, for example, of the various medi-

Table 6.2. Effects of Typology in Job Situations

Thinking Types	Feeling Types	Intuitive Types	Sensing Types
Are interested in people's feelings in an intellectual way	Are interested in people's actual feelings.	Perceive the possibilities.	Perceive the "facts."
Like logic and analysis.	Dislike logic and analysis.	Are impatient with routine details.	Are patient with routine details.
Decide impersonally, often ignoring people's actual feelings.	Decide on the basis of their own likes and wishes.	Follow inspirations.	Rarely trust inspirations.
Enjoy intellectual work.	Enjoy working with people.	Are careless about facts.	Seldom make errors of fact.
Like to adopt theories about how to manage.	Are quick to know their preferences.	Dislike precise work.	Are good at precise work.

cal specialties carried out by the Center for Applications of Psychological Type, Inc. demonstrate this. We know that few intuitives go into surgery. (And one can be grateful for that.) Similarly, very few sensation types go into psychiatry, which is largely made up of intuitives. In other specialties, there is more of a mixture depending on emphasis of one group of characteristics or the other.

In the corporation the same applies. Some positions require a developed sensation function, such as finance, accounting, and manufacturing. Marketing, on the other hand, requires sensation to sell, as well as intuition to develop new products and anticipate changes. In planning, thinking is necessary to link past and present to the future; a characteristic of thinkers is this kind of time-sense. In my testing, I have found, for example, the following characteristics:

Engineering.   Thinking and sensation.

Manufacturing.   Sensation and feeling. (Management of people is important here.)

Research and Development.   Thinking and intuition.

In the make-up of the task force, all of the typological characteristics should be present, with emphasis on that required by the nature of the task. If the leader can instill an attitude of tolerance and respect for all of the viewpoints being presented, rather than the usual competition, then better solutions will be reached in a more orderly fashion by all concerned.

Be prepared for a few surprises, however. In a study of the psychological typology of a sample of 333 certified public accountants for a doctoral dissertation, Philip F. Jacoby, working under Dr. Jerry B. Harvey of George

Washington University's Department of Management Science, found that in the accounting profession thinking combined with either sensation or intuition was the formula for success as measured by advancement in the firm. The overall picture emerging from Jacoby's research was that accounting is a profession which attracts a wide variety of types but is distinguished by a high proportion of thinkers, and especially introverted thinking types, with auxiliary sensation. But he also found that accountants were 53 percent introverts and 47 percent extroverts, a finding which contradicts the stereotype of the introverted accountant with the green eye shade and grim expression. However, as you would expect, there is a strong preference for thinking as a part of judgment among the accounting professionals.

TYPE AND THE BUSINESS LIFE CYCLE

There is a relationship between the type function requirements of effectively managing a business and the product or business life cycle. A business or product that is at the introductory stage of the life cycle is in a high growth, fast-changing situation. To successfully manage such a business, managers need to be sensitive to rapidly changing competitive moves and rapidly evolving customer perceptions of needs and wants. There is a requirement for intuitive vision to anticipate where the market is going.

As a business grows and the market matures, there is less demand for creativity and more for nuts and bolts management of a stabilized market and competitive field. The emphasis shifts from a premium for intuitive insight to a need for thinking and sensation in order to manage a stabilized business, as well as feeling to manage people. This change can present real problems for any company because the qualities that were necessary to establish a new enterprise may not necessarily be the qualities that are needed to manage a competitive mature market business.

The product portfolio model links the market share of a business with the rate of market growth. A business with low market share in a high-growth market is a question mark because, unless it can increase its market share, it will not be profitable. A star is a business with high market share in a high-growth market. Both of these businesses require intuition to anticipate the fast changes that go along with market development. The intuition might be combined with thinking or with feeling and, in the strong business, there will be both strong thinking and strong feeling.

As products mature, growth declines. The low-growth, high-share business is a cash cow because it is profitable and generates a surplus cash flow. The low-growth, low-share business is a "dog" because it is not profitable and does not generate a cash surplus. Both of these businesses need sensation more than intuition to manage the details and do the best possible job of giving people what they want. Attention to detail and thoroughness will pay off in these types of businesses.

The product portfolio and the relationship of the types of each of the four businesses is illustrated in Figure 6.1. Also illustrated in this figure is the relationship of each of the stages of the product life cycle to the critical requirements for success.

The reason that a company or product is developed in the first place is always related to the fact that an individual or a group backed an idea. The new product or business is the concrete expression of the idea, and the idea is a creative formulation of intuition.

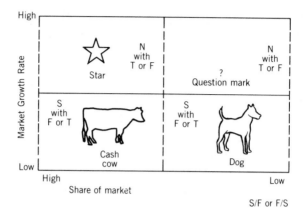

Figure 6.1. The product portfolio and type.

A business that goes from the introduction to the mature stage of its life is one that has been created by managers who have been able to focus initially on the task of taking an idea and from it creating a product and a business. If the business is to prosper in its maturity, it is important that respect and emphasis be given to the task of managing what exists and of serving customers.

Polaroid is a good example of a company that was created on the basis of a new idea: instant photography. The company grew and prospered on the basis of this idea, but the founder, Dr. Edwin H. Land, has remained in spirit an inventor committed to the development of ideas generated in the lab. His lack of interest in the task of serving customers, as opposed to developing the next idea, has limited the ability of Polaroid to generate sales and profits from its existing technology and production capacity.

Type theory does not suggest or lend support to the suggestion that Dr. Land should change his style, or his "spots." He is a creative genius, and that is wonderful. What type theory suggests is that Dr. Land might be more tolerant of those in his organization who want to manage a mature business and exploit the potential of Polaroid's technology and manufacturing capacity. This might mean getting into the components and materials business to exploit the potential of Polaroid battery and chemical processing technology. Dr. Land could still do what he likes to do, and do it as only he can do it. In his harsh pronouncements, insisting that Polaroid will not get significantly involved outside of its instant photography business, one can see more than a little of the intolerance of a highly differentiated intuitive for the "boring" work of the sensate.

The "triple threat" organization is, of course, one that manages programs at each stage of the life cycle, values each of the functions, and applies them as needed to each product and business.

ORGANIZATIONAL STYLES

Like individuals, organizations tend to develop styles. There are thinking organizations devoted to the latest theory of management, which tend to be cold, objective, and impersonal. There are intuitive style organizations that nurture ideas and creative insights; think tanks and the more successful advertising agencies have mastered this style. There are practical sensate style organizations that excel at doing repetitive things well and on time. A good example is the printing firm with the motto, "promises kept, deadlines met." Finally, there are organizations that have what could be called a feeling style; they may be absolutely world class in their mastery of the thinking, intuitive, and sensate side of their business, but their style has a strong feeling tone and orientation. An example of a highly successful, mature company that

practices a "feeling" style of management is Delta Airlines, widely regarded as one of the best managed, as
well as most profitable airlines. Delta treats its people
like members of a family. There have been, for example,
no layoffs in 25 years. The experience of this company
underlines the effectiveness of expressing feeling values
in creating organizations that really do perform.

Delta is a family. There is a commitment to the welfare
of Delta people that has generated great loyalty and
esprit de corps from the entire organization. Delta is a
very rich example of what a feeling attitude can do.
Along with its commitment to people, is a commitment
to running a nonunion airline, and they've been successful in this too. The result is that people can double
up jobs; there is no redundancy in work assignments
with the kind of work rules that run up labor costs.
What they have is a system that is similar to the Japanese
system and that also emphasizes feeling values. They're
actually more efficient because of it and because they're
more efficient, they can provide uninterrupted employment, superb benefits, and a happy working environment. In other words, it's working. The ticket taker
actually takes the ramp to the plane. Instead of three
people taking the plane out of the airstrip, one person
does it with a truck, and people are used efficiently and
not limited to a single task. Because the company is
more efficient, it is more profitable and the profits are
shared with employees. Delta's employee benefit plan is
one of the most generous in U.S. industry.

IBM is another example in the American business
culture of a company that expresses a feeling character
and philosophy. As we pointed out in the Introduction,
if you review the history of IBM under Thomas Watson,
you find that one of the things that was very distinctive
about that company was Watson's idea that it was a

family, along with his tremendous ability to express feeling values as a corporate policy. A family is something you don't expel people from for incompetence. A family is where people are connected, and this is true of IBM. They have a policy of, in effect, lifetime employment (similar to the Japanese model). You can be fired for "lack of sincerity," that is, for wearing a colored shirt on the job, for drinking, or for other forms of outrageous behavior in the plant or office. But if you were "sincere," mere incompetence would not be grounds for dismissal; you just wouldn't be promoted. It was, after all, a family.

This kind of environment may seem overly sentimental, but there is something of value here. And I think it was responsible for an organization that expresses a great deal of impressive marketing ability, and a tremendous awareness of the actual situation in the marketplace. There is also a lot of intuition in the company, some of it underground.

The alternative to this is an organization committed to profits first and people last. But one does not get profits because one is committed to profits; one gets them because one performs. Organizations perform when people are motivated and well managed to do their best. The paradox is that there is a bottom-line payoff in developing feeling function in companies and expressing that in organizational practices.

EXTROVERTED AND INTROVERTED STYLES

One way of looking at the way attitude and function relate to different types of job assignments is to see how these specifically affect behavior. There are certain tasks in an organization that demand an attitude of extroversion. It is absolutely essential that a salesperson relate to the object, the object being the customer. If the sales-person doesn't have available the capacity to be extro-verted, to actually see the other person, he or she is going to be in trouble.

Example: One of the most successful brokers in New York City regularly argued with customers who didn't agree with him. This would be a typically introverted way of relating to the customer. When he became aware of this (at an EST seminar), and consciously set out to change it, there was a dramatic difference in his per-formance. He had all the other skills in place, but his argumentativeness was a huge flaw.

By consciously making the effort to focus on the cus-tomer, actively listen to him or her, and accept the phi-losophy that the customer was right, he redefined his goal. He now sees it as that of meeting the needs of his customer, not reforming the customer. He has become very successful.

This is the essence of the marketing concept, based on the proposition that the focus of business should be on the customer and what the customer wants. Here is another example this time of an industry that ignored this precept and failed.

The situation of Detroit in the 1970s is one of typically introverted behavior in which the automobile manufac-turers tried to manipulate the customer into wanting the product. But, if you look at Detroit when it was success-ful, you will see a model of extroverted behavior. The manufacturers were attuned to the customer and gave them what they wanted. There were cheap gas and cheap steel: kids would buy a quarter's worth of gas and cruise around all evening. People wanted sexy, big cars. But the world changed and Detroit did not. It has consequently become a case history of catastrophe—because of introverted behavior when extroverted behavior was called for.

Detroit now faced a situation where quality and smallness were called for; for the first time the manufacturers faced competition in a whole new market. They were too introverted to see that quality was now important, as defined by fit, finish, appointment, and engineering finesse. Thus, the Japanese and the Germans beat them on these terms. Detroit manufacturers were also negatively affected by lack of intuition. The only thing that they could see was what was before them, and what was before them were cheap gas and a situation in which the United States was isolated from world problems and shortages. The United States, at that time, was the only country (together with Canada and Mexico) that did not treat gasoline as a scarce commodity and tax it accordingly. Detroit took this as a fact of life when, in fact, what was real was the law of supply and demand. They did not foresee that the macro forces of supply and demand were going to require a real adjustment to scarcity of materials and resources, and they didn't plan for it. They were thus cut off from reality. Their isolation cut off their intuition and their perception of reality through sensation. For example, their executives would drive a brand new car for a few thousand miles and then have it replaced. They never had the experience of running a car into the ground, as the consumer did, and seeing it fall apart. They also never paid for their own gas. They despised the funny-looking Volkswagen, without understanding why it was appealing to the consumer and that it was the harbinger of a totally new era in car design. Detroit manufacturers took an introverted attitude and "did it their way," thus isolating themselves from the subject, that is, the market.

But an organization can also succeed on the basis of an introverted attitude, where it is connected to a deep, inner value that is permanent and that relates to the needs and wants of the marketplace. There are two examples of successful introverted publishing businesses: *The New Yorker* and *Reader's Digest.* These magazines have grown and prospered through thick and thin because they have always had a connection to the values of their founders, who had a vision of what they should be and, in each case, the vision reflected a real and enduring market need.

These magazines have had the guidance of this "inner" direction to concentrate and focus their energy on what they do well, as opposed to constantly trying to adjust to the latest fashion. They have seen imitators come and go. Both of these magazines have what I call "soul." One way of seeing this is to compare current issues of either magazine to those of 40 or 50 years ago. They have on the surface changed very little; even the typefaces are almost the same. The "Talk of the Town" section in *The New Yorker* in the 1980s is remarkably (even consciously) like the "Talk of the Town" feature in the 1930s. This kind of reporting on life doesn't change that much because this side of life doesn't change that much. *Reader's Digest* of July 1936 had no advertising, but the articles carry titles like "The Coming Boom in Real Estate" (why house prices will soon shoot up), as compared to the June 1981 title "What Supply Side Economics Means to You." *Reader's Digest* has always published articles on money, sex, raising children, fears and concerns, hopes and aspirations, how to be happy and fulfilled, and the like. This is a list of subjects that will never go out of style.

These publications are introverted where it counts, but they are also extroverted where it counts, and that is really the theme of this book. Any one of these characteristics in isolation creates a distortion that will cause trouble. What one wants is balance, not necessarily in the individual, but in an organization made up of individuals with different type characteristics.

Reader's Digest, for example, has added advertising and has adapted in many ways to the market changes. *The New Yorker* continues to print fiction, cartoons, and essays that are interesting; it knows its market very well. It thus provides a magnificent forum for advertisers.

The basic desire of the people in Detroit was to make money, not to make cars, and that was a feeling decision. If you look at the people at the *Digest* or *The New Yorker*, you see people who are driven by another feeling quality: the desire to produce something that is the best.

Looking at new product development is a nice way to look at the relationship between attitude, function, and task. In the process of new product development are stages. In order to creatively identify the idea, there is a requirement for an unfettered creative intuition. It is very important at this stage to allow the intuition of people searching for ideas to range freely. It is pure perception that is required at this initial stage.

After the ideas have been generated, it becomes necessary to screen, to identify those ideas that will fit both the organization's capabilities and the needs of the market. This is a stage where facts are required, and this is a job for sensation. In the end, it will require some judgments, based not only on thinking but on feeling. Intuitiveness, so necessary to the idea generation stage, now has to be reined in as the organization focuses on the result through testing, prototype development, and all of the other things that are done to get the product on the market.

Once a prototype is in the test market, it is necessary to make a decision again about whether or not to go ahead. At this point, intuition may again emerge to make the decision to go ahead.

Many marketing executives are intuitives. This is a valuable function for seeing ahead and around the corner to the needs and wants of tomorrow. It is also a powerful function for perceiving the essence of a situation. The marketing vice-president of a large U.S. multinational corporation is an example of this style of marketing leadership. He has acute intuitive capacity and a forceful personality that enables him to successfully convey his holistic perceptions of the essence of a situation. He is currently preoccupied with the way in which quality has slipped in the United States and the consequent impact on sales. When he speaks to managers in the organization about quality, he uses a feeling conviction and also a sense of the holistic aspect of quality as it affects the company. That is an intuitive quality, and he is extremely persuasive. He catches the essence of what is critical for advancing the organization toward its goals and, in that, reflect a very powerful intuition. One is also impressed with his absolutely inferior sensation. This is the kind of man who will lose a car registration and, as a solution, will simply rent a car for an extended period of time—because he can't find the registration for his own car. This is also a man who left a $12,000 check on somebody's desk; whose expense accounts are four or five months late all the time. He is a combination of a very powerful intuition and a sensation function that is weak or, under stress, nonexistent.

This executive is making a great contribution to his organization in spite of the fact that he is not on top of the details that only a developed sensate can perceive. In the case of his organization, the size and degree of specialization make it unnecessary for him to be on top of such details. In a smaller organization, he would be a disaster as a marketing vice-president because there would be no one around to look after the day-to-day selling and administration. This underlines the difficulty of generalizing about the relationship between type and task in business. One could say that marketing executives should be intuitives: either intuitive thinkers or thinking intuitives. But there are organizations or levels in organizations where the most important task is not anticipating what is coming, what will happen next, or what the organization ought to be preparing for, but rather selling what the organization produces and doing an outstanding job of servicing customer accounts. This requires sensation, and this is part of marketing. Thus, you can see, one cannot generalize about function and task. Most business functions, and certainly general management, are broad enough to require all of the functions in order to be effective.

CONCLUSION

Even though it is often comfortable to be with people who are of the same type as ourselves, the key to organizational excellence is type complementarity. This complementarity can only be created by making a conscious effort because, left to our "natural" tendencies, we will tend to choose people who are like ourselves to join our team. The result of making the effort to create a complementary team is well worth the effort, for only when each of the functions and attitudes is represented can we be sure that we are giving the fullest possible attention to the organization's reality.

7

Intuition, Creativity, and the Gut Reaction

I make all my decisions on intuition. But then, I must know why I made that decision. I throw a spear into the darkness. That is intuition. Then I must send an army into the darkness to find the spear. That is intellect.

INGMAR BERGMAN[1]

Intuition, according to the Swedish film director Ingmar Bergman, is the essence of creativity and the foundation of his unparalleled success as a filmmaker. It is a leap into the unknown and springs from the depths of the unconscious. It is holistic perception, or what is often called the sixth sense, in contrast to the five ordinary senses that make up the sensation function. According to the dictionary, intuition is "the act or faculty of knowing without the use of rational processes; immediate cognition." The word *intuition* comes from the

[1]"Ingmar Bergman Confides in Students," *The New York Times*, May 8, 1981, p. C7.

129

Latin *intueri*, to look at or toward, to contemplate: *in-*, on, toward, combined with *tueri*, to look at, watch.[2]

Creativity requires the insight of intuition. Everyone in the advertising business knows this, even those who lack a real intuitive talent. Intuition is fragile, and it takes guts to trust it because you can't put your hands on its source. It's not like the world of hard facts that many executives feel quite uncomfortable without. John Elliott, Jr., a statesman in the advertising industry, on the occasion of his retirement told his fellow workers at Ogilvy Mather International about his early employment as a copywriter at Batten, Barton, Durstine & Osborne: "I was pretty good, but not good enough," he said. "I could execute campaigns, but I never came up with big ideas. So I went into a less demanding line of work. I became an account man. Ever since, I have stood in awe of people who could come up with big campaign ideas." He then added, "Big ideas are so hard to recognize, so fragile, so easy to kill. Don't forget that, all of you who don't have them."[3]

Elliott's comments contain two profound insights: first, his own self-knowledge—"I was pretty good, but not good enough." By accepting his own nature, he went on to be one of the best account executives in the business and to a life of real satisfaction and joy. He said, at his retirement dinner, "I love the advertising business. It has been very good to me. More than anything else, I have loved being able to say for 17 years, 'I am chairman of Ogilvy Mather'." These are not the words of a frustrated writer. They are the words of a top account executive. Thus, it is essential for each of us to accept our-

---

[2]*American Heritage Dictionary of the English Language*, Houghton Mifflin Company, Boston, 1976.
[3]*The New York Times*, December 16, 1981, p. D18.

selves; surely we all have our typological strengths and weaknesses. You cannot be what you want to be, you can only be what you are. If you will be just that, you will discover that you're OK, that you're better than OK, that you're perfect just as you are.

The next insight in these comments is Elliott's sensitivity to the fragility of creative ideas. They are easy to crush and kill, yet so hard to recognize. One of the essential requirements in the agency business is that the people who manage the agencies have the ability to provide a place where people can be creative. This is why we have advertising agencies in the first place. If this weren't so, clients could save the commissions and fees and do their own ads in house. But they can't, precisely because they typically do not create the atmosphere or climate that nurtures creativity.

Elliott's attitude toward creativity is one that every organization should strive to emulate. Every organization needs creativity, and the potential for creativity is always there. It only needs to be valued and recognized in order to be expressed.

HOW TO DEVELOP YOUR INTUITION

Now that you have completed Chapters 1–6, you are probably saying to yourself, "Well, so what? I know what's so if I believe the theory of types, but what do I do about it?" This chapter is the first of two that focus on developing intuition and feeling—the two functions lacking in most businesspeople.

One of the first things to recognize about intuition is that it is not about the trees, but rather, about the forest, about seeing the whole. In history, for example, it is the ability to see the place of myth in historical perspective. William H. McNeil commented on this recently:

> Historians' assaults on myth are themselves based on a myth: the faith that facts speak for themselves, that infinite detail somehow organizes itself into meaningful patterns without the intervention of human intelligence, and that historical truth resides in faithful transcription of recorded words and deeds.
> Few if any historians really believe these doctrines today, yet the practice of the profession mummified by Ph.D. training programs routinely perpetuates the writing of research monographs whose only point is to show that no one has quite managed to find a formula that could fully take into account newly noticed details.[4]

Intuition expresses itself in fantasy, dreams, visions, daydreams, and symbols. Encouraging these activities opens up the flow of intuition. There are four basic methods of encouraging, nudging, tickling, and growing your intuition.

1. Sense deprivation: Put yourself in a situation where there are as little sensory data as possible. Eliminate all sound, reading material, visual stimuli, orders, food, and, insofar as possible, even a sense of the temperature being too hot or cold. Then, just let your mind go completely blank. Try to avoid any thinking, and concentrate your intuition on anything in your life that intuition might be able to illuminate. Should you hire X for the product manager's job? Or, would Y be more effective in this position? You have all the facts, you have your own perception of the two finalists' appearance and character, and so on. You have thought through

---

[4]*The New York Times*, December 28, 1981, p. A19.

the situation from A to Z, but what you haven't done is really let your intuition take part in the decision process.

Intuition should not be allowed to *make* the decision. You must use your thinking or your feeling to decide whether to go with your intuition in this or in any situation. It is a mistake to assume that you can avoid responsibility for making decisions and choices by developing your intuition. What intuition can do for you is add more data. What it cannot do is rationally choose. The only rational functions are thinking and feeling.

One of the ways to tap your intuitive power is to read less. Ask yourself if you are getting anything out of your current level of reading (or TV-watching, or whatever you do to use your time). Chances are that you could cut back on an activity without any sacrifice of value. For years I read magazines like *Business Week* and *Forbes* until I realized that reading them from cover to cover was a real waste of time because the articles were repeating themselves. They were, in fact, just the same thing over and over again.

2.   Never hire someone or start a new project without an intuitive OK. If someone looks great on paper, looks presentable, and so on, but you feel an intuitive "no," keep looking. Perhaps your intuition is telling you that you can find a more qualified person, or perhaps it is telling you something about the person you are looking at. If it is the former, you need to carry on with your search. If it is the latter, you need to get more information. You should either get an intuitive OK or continue to gather information until you are satisfied that the candidate is the right one.

3.   Never confide in someone who you have reason to doubt is a real friend. Your intuition can be a real guide around the false smile, the ulterior motive, even the evil intention. If your intuition tells you to be on your guard,

listen to it. A friend is someone who is for you, not against you. A friend wishes you well and accepts you as you are. A friend helps you discover who you really are. If your intuition tells you that someone who seems to be a friend is not really a friend, then listen to that message. There are people who are your friends, and they are the ones you can confide in. If your intuition tells you that a person you were once wary of is actually OK, then you can go with the new signal, but until then be wary and cautious.

4.   Rely on your senses to pick up the trends, but rely on your intuition to sniff out the changes in trends. And, as Peter Drucker says, it is the changes in trends that we must be wary of, not the trends themselves.

"Sadat," said Henry Kissinger in a moving eulogy to Anwar Sadat, "was a very great man who made the difficult seem effortless. The difference between great and ordinary leaders is rarely formal intellect but insight."[5] Another word for insight, or inner sight, is intuition; and intuition is the key ingredient in creativity. Kissinger then goes on to give a description of creativity:

> The great (creative) man understands the essence of a problem; the ordinary leader grasps only the symptoms. The great man focuses on the relationship of events to each other; the ordinary leader sees only a series of seemingly disconnected events. The great man has a vision of the future that enables him to place obstacles into perspective; the ordinary leader turns pebbles in the road into boulders. [Creativity also involves the other functions: thinking and feeling and the sensation that allows action.] But a statesman must never be viewed as

[5]*Time Magazine*, October 19, 1981, p. 32.

starry eyed. He must have vision and depth; he must also translate his intuition into reality against sometimes resistant material.[6]

Everyone is born with his or her own potential for creativity. Studies of right brain–left brain development reveal a correlation in the left half of the brain with the thinking, rational, and linear functions, and in the right half, a correlation with intuitive, creative, and holistic function. Robert Ornstein, author of *The Psychology of Consciousness* and *The Mind Field*, and editor of *The Nature of Human Consciousness*, has pioneered in right–left brain studies. He is fond of using Sufi stories, moralistic parables like those used by Jesus and Aesop, to show how Eastern cultures educate children "holistically" by exposing them to the complexity of life through stories. This contrasts with Western specialization. Thus, in the Sufi story, the child is given a description of human behavior, a story to entertain, and a moral to think about. In the West, learning would be fragmented into linear, specialized curricula. A consequence of this is the idea that people "specialize." Jim is an artist, therefore he is "creative." Mary is a mathematician, therefore she is a "thinker." In reality, both may or may not be creative; creativity is a capacity that we are born with, that some lose, and that some develop in line with genetic make-up. The idea that creativity is a function available to everyone is a comparatively new one. Einstein was a "creative" physicist in that he was able to "create" a new idea, that is, the theory of relativity. Some artists are never anything but derivative. As Kissinger said, this creative orientation can also be expressed in

---

[6]Ibid.

government or almost any kind of human activity, including business.

THE CREATIVE TENSION

Jung's fascination with the tension of opposites—between instinct and spirit (or archetypal image), conscious and unconscious, shadow and light, extrovert and introvert—is a basic preoccupation of the creative personality. Arthur Rothenberg, a professor of psychiatry and behavioral science at the University of Connecticut Health Center and clinical professor of psychiatry at the Yale School of Medicine, has conducted extensive studies and interviews with writers, artists, and scientists that reveal this preoccupation with polarities he calls "Janusian thinking," after the double-faced Greek god. He describes how paradox played a part in Einstein's discovery of the theory of relativity (two objects falling at the same speed will be at rest in relation to each other), and in Watson's discovery of the nature of the double helix (identical but spatially opposed chains).

Rothenberg has observed that writers, including Eugene O'Neill and Joseph Conrad (*Nostromo*), creatively used paradox in their greatest work, as did Picasso in his masterpiece "Guernica." Over a period of 15 years, Rothenberg studied and interviewed 54 recognized artists and scientists in the United States and England. At the same time, Rothenberg interviewed a "control group" of successful people who were not considered to be creative by others. These were asked to write a piece of imaginative fiction, such as poems and short stories.

Janusian thinking seldom appears in the final artistic product, but it occurs at critical points in the generation and development of the work. In the initial phase of interviews with some of the writers, they reported using numerous opposite ideas, images, and concepts, but there were usually no clues at that point to the importance of their ideas. . . . It was generally only after weeks or months of interviewing and the development of confidence and rapport that the research subjects revealed the precise and contradictory nature of the critical ideas in their creation.[7]

Some of these were:

A novel about a revolutionary hero who, responsible for hundreds of deaths, would kill only one person himself, "and this was the one who had been very kind to him and the one person he loved."

A play that would "simultaneously express both the beauty of modern Germany and Hitler's destructiveness."

A poem expressing the dual nature of rocks, the sensuous touch of their surface and the lethal potential of their weight, which "led to a conception of the simultaneous operation of sex and violence in the world."

A novel showing that "love and hate were the same."

A poem made up of a series of lines that used the last word of each line as the first word of the next.

However, Rothenberg found that although such "Janusian thinking" occurred throughout his investigation of creative people, "the controls never displayed it in their thoughts or in any aspect of the writing assign-

[7]Albert Rothenberg, "Creative Contradictions," *Psychology Today,* June 1979, pp. 52–62.

ment they were asked to do. . . . Their earliest conceptions, and those along the way, were devoid of simultaneous antithesis."[8]

Rothenberg also did a statistical analysis of the manu-
scripts of such famous authors as Eugene O'Neill, Max-
well Anderson, and Stephen Vincent Benet, developing
specific predictions about their work. He also interviewed
surviving relatives to assess his predictions. With respect to Joseph Conrad, for example, he found that
Conrad followed a Janusian sequence in *Nostromo*.
Conrad described this sequence in the preface. He was
struck by a story he had heard about an "unmitigated
rascal" who had stolen a large quantity of silver somewhere on the seaboard of South America during a revo-
lution. "I did not see anything at first in the mere story,"
he recalled. Then, he said, "It dawned upon me that the
purloiner of the treasure need not necessarily be a confirmed rogue, that he could even be a man of character."
This key idea of the criminal as both rogue and man of
character was elaborated on in the story of a land that was
both good and evil simultaneously. As Conrad reported,

> It was only then that I had the first vision of a twilight
> country . . . with . . . its high, shadowy sierra and its
> misty camp for mute witnesses of events flowing from
> the passions of men shortsighted in good and evil. Such
> are in very truth the obscure origins of Nostromo—the
> book. From that moment I suppose, it had to be.[9]

This cognitive phenomenon can be compared to ideas
inherent in Eastern religions, such as Taoism, with its
concept of yin and yang as two opposite and universal
principles that join together to create a single force, for

[8]Ibid., p. 59.
[9]Ibid., p. 59.

example, male/female. Another such religion is Buddhism, in which nirvana, the end of the cycle of rebirth, is at once opposed to and unified with samsara, the reincarnation of living things. In Western theology, there is the similar tension occurring in the concept of God and the devil. Just as Freud postulated the conscious—unconscious relationship, so did Jung carry it forward to the conscious–shadow and the juxtaposition of "animus"—the hidden male in the female, and "anima"—the hidden female in the male.

Rothenberg also points out that this creative use of opposites is not merely the association of two incompatible elements, but an intentional choice of opposites. "Clearly, bringing together any opposites at all won't do . . . the creator chooses and develops these opposites and antithesis that most meaningfully crystallize and express personal as well as universal values, experiences and feelings." He continues:

> Always surprising is the discovery that the opposite of a previously held idea, concept or belief is operative or true. Even more surprising is this: not only is the opposite true, but *both* the opposite and the previously held idea are operative or true. Nothing could jar our expectations more.[10]

CUSTER AND THE BATTLE OF THE LITTLE BIG HORN: A CASE OF INTUITIVE MYOPIA

The battle of the Little Big Horn was an engagement between the Seventh Cavalry commanded by Lieutenant Colonel Armstrong Custer and Sioux and Cheyenne led by Sitting Bull, Crazy Horse, Gall, and others.

[10]Ibid., p. 62.

Colonel Custer was part of a coordinated effort of the U.S. Army to force the native Americans back onto their reservation. He was under the command of Brigadier General Terry, who had ordered him to keep his main force available south of the Little Big Horn as part of a plan to surround the Indians, who were thought to be on the Little Big Horn River. Instead of following his instructions not to march too rapidly, on the morning of the 25th of June, 1876, Custer was overlooking the Little Big Horn. He saw a small force of warriors, but unfortunately, the Indian camp on the west bank of the river was much larger than Custer realized because the terrain hid a large portion of the Indian encampment from his view. In fact, the encampment consisted of 12,000 to 15,000 Indians, including 4,000 to 5,000 warriors. Custer apparently intended to attack at dawn on the 26th of June. However, erroneous information that his presence had been discovered led him to a decision to attack immediately, even though his men and horses were exhausted from the long day's ride.

Custer divided his command of 650 men and led a group of 225 men down a small valley toward the river where they were annihilated by the overwhelmingly superior Indian force.

I would describe Custer typologically as a sensate with inferior intuition. When he rode up the valley and saw the small Indian force, what he saw was what he saw. Of course, what he didn't see was the entire Sioux and Cheyenne nation beyond his line of sight. His intuition, that sense of the possibility in a situation, simply did not operate at that particular moment. Extroverted sensates have in common their willingness to respond quickly to external stimuli and are oriented toward action rather than reflection and introspection. Extroverted sensates are present oriented and have an almost total lack of concern with past or future; their whole orientation is to respond without hesitation to environmental stimuli. They do not need to wait to incorporate additional information into their response pattern. Of course, for Custer, his inferior or unconscious intuition was a fatal weakness. Had he exercised intuition or listened to intuition at that moment of decision to attack, history might have been recorded differently.[11]

MATCHING TYPE TO SELF

A classic intuitive creative type is the inventor Robert W. Lester, who holds 50 U.S. patents and figures he's one of a dwindling breed of approximately 100 American inventors. As has been reported, Lester gets bored with his inventions as soon as he has created them. "When I finish an invention," he is quoted as saying, "even before I finish writing the patent application, I'm not interested in it anymore. I'm interested in new things."[12] This is the voice of a real intuitive speaking. He is simply bored with following through on anything. He's an interesting example of this typology because he has enough talent to support himself handsomely from his royalties and he just wants to keep on inventing. In this case, Lester is not worried about his typological weakness; he's sticking to his strengths and has structured his life and work around them. Lester's intuitive approach to

[11]*Report for the Secretary of War*, Vol. 1, 1876; communicated to the 44th Congress, Second Session, pp. 439–448; 476–480. I am indebted to Neil L. Halliday, Jr. for his report, "The Courtmartial of George Armstrong Custer: A Critical Analysis," which suggested this example.

[12]Gregory Swith, "It's Better Than Chasing Girls," *Forbes*, December 10, 1979, pp. 85–89.

life works for him. His experience underlines the fact that there is no "right" way to develop typologically.

The best typological development depends upon the needs of the individual and the needs of the job. In Lester's case, his goals in life were more than fulfilled by his vocation of inventing, and the actual work itself could be done by relying principally on his intuitive capacity. Another example of a creative genius who was not balanced in his typological development is Albert Einstein. Einstein discovered the theory of relativity, but he did not know what color his socks were, and he did not have a great deal of warmth in his relationships with people. His "feeling" was for the whole human race, rather than for individual humans. And yet, who would argue that he should have been more balanced? Clearly, he developed in a way that allowed him to meet his own goals in life, or, as a more religious person might say, he found his own soul.

Managers, unlike men like Lester and Einstein, cannot so easily succeed on a single function. The task of management requires all four functions, so managers need to be more typologically balanced in order to perform their jobs effectively. Many tasks require all four functions in order to be effectively accomplished. The structural collapse of large buildings or sections of them often results from a lack of attention to less "interesting," grubby details such as type and number of supports, connections, washers, or welds. This attention requires the sensation function.

Indeed, one of the problems with America's ability to compete in the world economy in manufacturing is the inadequate attention to and development of the sensation function. To put it another way, in our thinking-intuitive-oriented culture, we have difficulty in giving attention to small details. The poor differentiation of sensation is responsible for our poor performance in this area.

ALEX F. OSBORN'S STUDIES

According to Alex F. Osborn[13] there are four mental functions:

1. The absorptive—the ability to observe and to apply attention (equals sensation)
2. The retentive—the ability to memorize and recall (equals feeling)
3. The reasoning—the ability to analyze and judge (equals thinking)
4. The creative—the ability to visualize, foresee, and generate ideas (equals intuition)

The first three functions can be performed by computers.

The fourth, or creative, imaginative, intuitive function is a human gift that is universally distributed. Indeed, this capacity is lying fallow in most people, just waiting for the opportunity to express itself. Sometimes it takes an external threat to mobilize creative energy. World War II was a time when Americans mobilized overnight and did the impossible. The country went from a Depression to a period of incredible feats of production and invention under the threat of the Axis powers to the American way of life and ideals. The same kind of creative burst occurs in the lives of individuals and

[13]Alex F. Osborn, *Applied Imagination*, 3rd ed. (New York: Charles Scribner's Sons, 1963).

companies when there is a market challenge to be met or when there is a willingness to take the risks that go with the creative leap.

Creativity is not a monopoly of youth. Oliver Wendell Holmes published *Autocrat at the Breakfast Table* around the age of 50. He wrote his famed biography of Ralph Waldo Emerson at 75. Thomas Jefferson "retired" at age 66 to Monticello and was highly creative thereafter, still inventing in his seventies and eighties. Benjamin Franklin wrote his great appeal to Congress for the abolition of slavery at 84. Osborn reports that Professor Harvey C. Lehman of Ohio University studied a group of 1,000 "notables" who have produced ideas of importance. The median age at which these achievements occurred was 74.

DEVELOPING YOUR CREATIVITY CAPACITY

Creativity can be developed by exercising the intuitive function of the mind.

There are many ways to do this. A few examples are:

1. Gain experience firsthand. Travel. Talk to people who are doing things that interest you.
2. Play games and solve puzzles.
3. Participate in hobbies and the fine arts.
4. Read.
5. Write.
6. Practice solving problems.
7. Cut out cartoons from a magazine; remove the captions and think of new ones.
8. Select famous works of art and create new titles.

The creative problem solving process involves three steps:

Step 1.   Fact finding
Step 2.   Idea finding
Step 3.   Solution finding

This was the creative pattern of Bernard Baruch: he got the facts, studied them carefully, and then applied his imagination. He would also review what additional information he needed and, in seeking this new information, also used his imagination. Alex Osborn warns us that facts may swamp the imagination. He suggests the use of inductive reasoning: think of all the possible hypotheses that would explain the situation or phenomenon.

In successful problem solving, it is important to discriminate between those problems requiring creative ideas and those requiring value judgments. Take, for example, the decision about whether or not to go into a new business. First, there is the value judgment: do we want to expand the present business into new fields? If the answer to this question is yes, then you must solve the creative problem of how to do it. For example, a company might find it desirable to develop a new product or change the existing one to meet changing tastes in consumer demand. There must be a judgment made about changing the product. Once this is tested and evaluated, and the decision made, there are then the creative problems of positioning, naming, and marketing the new or revised product.

Creativity is basically the finding of new connections between old or existing facts. The mind is like a computer data file where there are millions of bits of knowledge and information stored. When someone finds a new relationship or pattern, she or he is being creative. More an art than a science, creativity must tap into the unconscious, bypassing the conscious thinking functions. Therefore, it is hard to consciously will oneself to be "creative"; if it's there, it comes—through day and night dreams, fantasies, and what are called "inspirations." There are certain times when the unconscious is more likely to surface; on awakening in the morning, for example. Try taking a few moments each morning to lie quietly in a period of "creative silence" before the day intrudes on your mind, and concentrate on being receptive to whatever ideas pop into your head.

IDEA-GENERATING METHODS

In generating ideas, it is important to defer judgment and generate as many alternatives as possible. A good maxim for ideation is "quantity breeds quality." Collaboration can stimulate individual creativity by supporting the climate of openness. It is not only other people who pass judgment on our ideas. We often rain on our own parade. When there is a group effort or group support, this can silence the voices within that say things like "that won't work," or "that's a ridiculous idea, you can't do it," and so on.

Some commonly used methods of generating ideas are:

1. *Brainstorm.* Essentially, this involves getting a group of people together to generate ideas. The essence of brainstorming is the suspension of judgment, that is, the suspension of thinking and feeling. Thinking and feeling evaluate and judge ideas, and the purpose of brainstorming is to generate ideas, not judge them. The

combination of the suspension of judgment and the energy that can come from group enthusiasm, commitment, and sharing makes this a powerful tool for idea generation or ideation. The rules of brainstorming are simple: (1) Obtain a quantity, not quality, of ideas. (2) Do not judge or evaluate ideas until all the ideas are presented because judgments kill ideas and therefore are only allowed after all the ideas are in. (3) Encourage the far out, unusual, weird, and impractical—anything goes. (4) Encourage group members to piggyback on the ideas of others by adding new features. (5) Explore every aspect of the broadest possible approach to a problem. (For example, if a new can opener is required, explore the different aspects of openness.) (6) Force relationships between two or more normally unrelated products or ideas as a starting point for generating ideas. (7) List the attributes of an object or idea, and then look for the relationships between the attributes. (8) Record ideas as they occur; carry note cards and use a bedside pad for writing down notes and ideas. (9) Look at solutions others have found and try to adapt these to the problem at hand. This was Edison's approach. Examples of this are taking an idea like the Book of the Month Club and adapting it to records, fruit, cheese, and so on. Most games are adaptations of existing games. Baseball was adapted from the English game called rounders, and football was adapted from rugby. Racquetball was adapted from handball and squash, and a new game called Porchball was adapted from racquetball. The only original American game is basketball.

2. *Capture Your Ideas.* There is a relationship between creativity and the emotions; people think better when they are not depressed or tired. A key to the development of creativity is effort, concentration, and a good night's sleep. Take notes of any ideas that appear. Ralph Waldo Emerson knew how easy it is to lose a thought. He advised, "Look sharply after your thoughts. They come unlooked for like a new bird seen on your trees, and, if you turn to your usual task, disappear."

DEVELOPING YOUR CREATIVITY THROUGH GAMES

All of the people who have studied creativity agree: being creative requires the preservation of the curiosity and sense of wonder that you had as a child. Unfortunately, this is the one quality that is absent from most adults. Jean Piaget, the famous French psychologist, put it this way, "If you want to be creative, stay in part a child, with the creativity and invention that characterizes children before they are deformed by adult society." Children love to play and invent games. These qualities of play and invention are something we should all strive to preserve.

To help develop creativity, psychologist Eugene Raudsepp has developed a set of games that require mental flexibility and the ability to move out of old patterns of so-called "logical" thinking.[14] The characteristics of the creative person, according to Raudsepp, are:

1. Awareness of the possibility of alternative solutions, for example, imagination
2. Ability to find simple unobvious solutions
3. Ability to make a correct hypothesis from a few bits of data or clues
4. Ability to visualize

[14]Eugene Raudsepp and George P. Hough, Jr., *Creative Growth Games* (New York: Harcourt Brace Jovanovich, 1977).

5. A "predisposition to think in opposites" (Raud-sepp says creative people in word association tests consistently give antonyms)

6. Ability to perceive similarities and differences between objects

7. Visual acuity

A typical and excellent example is the old problem of dots and straight lines.

GETTING OUT OF THE BOX

Draw four straight lines through these nine dots without retracing or lifting your pencil from the paper.

• • •
• • •
• • •

A typical attempt looks like this:

In fact, the solution is easy, if you get out of the box. (See the end of this chapter.) What makes it impossible for people to solve this puzzle is that they create a box, an invisible barrier around the dots. No one else does this, and it is not in the directions! You do this to yourself.

CONCLUSION

Intuition is a function of the mind, and creativity is an act that draws especially on this function. Typologically, we are all born with the potential to exercise our creative facilities, but unless we have relied primarily on our intuitive function, the chances are that we suppress it in order to use the other functions. This chapter has suggested ways you can stimulate and revive your own creative/intuitive powers. All the methods suggested in this chapter involve a simple but fundamental rule: to develop your intuition, you must use it, and to use it, you must suppress the other functions, especially your sensate perception of what's so, but also your thinking and feeling judgment, which tells you that the great idea you have is silly and will never work. Of course, the thinking and feeling may be correct 99 times out of 100, but the creative breakthrough comes of the hundredth idea. This is why quantity is so important in the creative process.

SOLUTION TO THE BOX

8

Feeling: The Critical Difference

Feeling is primarily a process that takes place between the ego and a given content, a process, moreover, that imparts to the content a definite value in the sense of acceptance or rejection ("like" or "dislike").

C. G. JUNG
(PSYCHOLOGICAL TYPES, P. 434)

INTRODUCTION

In this chapter, we shift our attention from intuition, a function of perception, to feeling, one of the judging functions. Feeling and intuition have one important thing in common: they are both "right-brain" functions. That is to say, they both are holistic as opposed to linear, soft as opposed to hard, feminine as opposed to masculine, night as opposed to day. As such, they are somewhat neglected in our patriarchal culture, although there is a growing recognition of their importance. Of the two overlooked functions, perhaps the most critical to the success of the enterprise is feeling, the subject of this chapter.

The West has lost something of real value that it once had, and that is the feeling for creation, for work itself. A Japanese builder who recently visited the United States and the United Kingdom put it very well:

> People talk about the British disease and now the American disease, but it clearly wasn't always like that. Look at the care that went into the building of those old Victorian houses in London or the riveting on those big iron bridges they used to build in the United States. Even in Japan we don't see craftmanship like that. And you can tell just by looking that it was something that came naturally; workers did not have to be bribed or forced to produce it.[1]

The Japanese emphasis on what can be called the "feeling function" has contributed to their success. In the West, it is fair to say that most business executives shun or play down "feelings," at least when it comes to business decisions. We expect our decision-makers to be "hard-nosed" and rational, to think their way through problems and take action. Feelings are best left to artists and therapists.

The power of decisions that incorporate feeling is in their implementation. An organization is a collective, and Japanese managers recognize this fact. There is no myth of the Superman, or the leader who is responsible

[1]Gregory Clark, "The People Are the Enterprise," *PHP*, December 1981, p. 54.

for making everything happen. Instead, there is a realistic appreciation of the fact that every member of an organization contributes to its performance and should, therefore, participate in the rewards of its success.

In the West, by contrast, "thinking" dominates organizational decision-making. The overvaluation of thinking downgrades feeling and leads to decisions that do not really incorporate the full potential of the creative energy of all of the organization members. And, since decisions do not take into account the feelings of all organization members, leaders often find that there is overt agreement and covert subversion, or outright "stonewalling" by executives and workers who are focused on defensive guardianship of their power and "turf." This defensive behavior is largely a consequence of fear, and the fear is well grounded. By ignoring feelings, one ignores basic concerns and values, and people are guided and influenced by their concerns and values.

CASE EXAMPLE: UNCONSCIOUS FEELING

One of the most dramatic ways of underlining the importance of feeling in creating an effective leadership style is to look at what can happen when feeling is not present in a leader or chief executive officer. Donald Kircher, the late CEO of the Singer Company, is an example of an executive whose leadership style was based on extroverted thinking, auxiliary intuition, and what appeared to be relatively undeveloped or inferior feeling. In addition, his personality was aggressive and assertive. The combination of personality and type results in what I call a *Führer* or Superman style of leadership.

In 1958, Singer was 105 years old.[2] The company was rich in tradition and for most of its existence had been an impressive success as a one-product company. In the latter part of the company's first century, however, things had not gone so well. In 1920, Singer was ranked among the 20 largest U.S. companies. In 1958, Singer had dropped out of the top 100. In 1958, 95 percent of $446 million in sales was in sewing machines, a market that was severely threatened by competition from Germany and Japan, whose lower costs, lower prices, and more innovative designs had enabled them to push Singer's share of the U.S. market from 80 percent to 30 percent. The company was not cost competitive; U.S. operations were barely breaking even, and total earnings were down to a mere $10 million.

In 1958, the Board decided to promote Donald P. Kircher from his position as Vice-President for Legal Affairs to Chairman and Chief Executive Officer. Kircher was acknowledged by all to be an audacious and brilliant man. He had graduated with honors from Harvard College and Harvard Law School, and had a distinguished war record as a company commander serving under General Patton. He was a man of action, of intellect, and

[2]Background on the Singer Company is drawn from the following sources: "Whatever Happened to Singer?" *Forbes*, August 1, 1971, pp. 31–33; "Singer," *Forbes*, October 15, 1964, pp. 20–24; "It's a Spryer Singer," *Fortune*, December 1963, pp. 145–147; "How the Directors Kept Singer Stitched Together," *Fortune*, December 1975, pp. 100–109; "Flavin's Master Plan for Ailing Singer," *Business Week*, May 10, 1976, p. 66. I would also like to acknowledge an unpublished paper by Herbert Adams for my course, Business Policy Determination: "Strategy Formulation, a Critical Analysis of Organizational Practice: The Case of Singer Company, 1958–1975 under Chairman and Chief Executive Donald P. Kircher," April 19, 1977.

of enormous energy and ambition. He was determined to restore Singer to its former position of greatness.

In addition to the decline of market share and earnings, Kircher inherited a company with a tired, backward, and demoralized management. The worldwide sewing machine market was saturated and mature, and the company suffered from what was termed an embarrassment of riches: its past success had allowed it to build up a fortress of cash, marketable securities, land, and buildings far in excess of what it could profitably use in its business. The company stock was selling at half its book value. Kircher was determined to restore Singer to its former greatness. He said, in 1971:

> This was a great company once, one of the largest in America, but by the late fifties, it had enormously lost position. It was out of character for Singer simply to be one among many smaller companies. My job has been that of restoring the greatness of this enterprise.[3]

To do this, Kircher adopted a two-phased strategy. The first phase was to restore the market position, competitive strength, and profitability of the sewing machine business. Kircher began by selling the company's venerable old headquarters in the Wall Street area and moving the headquarters to Rockefeller Center. To suggest his vision of the future, modern abstract paintings replaced the old gilt-framed portraits from Singer's past. He then invested in manufacturing and began to expand production of smaller machines to better utilize Singer's company-owned distribution. He added a full line of modern appliances. Outlets were moved from downtown to malls. He hired new managers and made

[3]Whatever Happened to Singer?" p. 31.

room for them by firing and early retirement. He established a program of executive development through transfer and job rotation.

Phase One programs reversed the declining share of market and restored profitability to the sewing machine business. Kircher then launched Phase Two, a diversification program. The retail store product line was extended to include appliances, typewriters, televisions, and so on. A mail-order company was purchased. To round out the industrial sewing machine business, three companies were purchased; one made hosiery knitting machinery, the second, carpet tufting machinery, and the third, apparel knitting equipment. Space age technology was an acquisition target. Singer purchased Haller, Raymond & Brown (military infra-red cameras). The Metrics Division was created by acquiring three firms that manufactured spectrum analyzers, volt meters, and equipment that measured radio interference.

The results of Kircher's first four years were impressive. Sales rose 42 percent, and earnings were up 250 percent. In the sewing machine business, U.S. share of market increased 10 percent to 40 percent, and worldwide market shares rose from 20 percent to 25 percent. Singer even captured 10 percent of the Japanese market! The diversification program was a success. Operations outside sewing machines accounted for 21 percent of total sales and 25 percent of total earnings.

Flushed with success, Kircher shifted to Phase Three of his grand design, which was to move into high-growth areas. His policy was to find companies that would relate to Singer's strengths and expertise in manufacturing small precision machines and in marketing.

Kircher was determined to get into high-growth markets and was willing to accept high risk for the potential rewards. He chose the data processing field, fully realizing that all companies for sale in this area were unprofitable divisions with which other companies had failed.

In the spring of 1963, Friden was acquired for $175 million, or about 30 times earnings. There were immediate problems. First, in rotary calculators, the division's main product, there was still competition from Litton's Monroe Division and SCM's Marchant. Second, the division's new postage meters were promising, but Pitney-Bowes' 85 percent share of market seemed to be holding. Third, the division's peripheral equipment for computers was meeting increased competition from IBM.

Singer's total sales with Fridens were $800 thousand, with one-third now outside the traditional nonsewing-machine business. Kircher continued his extension of products sold in company retail stores, adding new items, such as home entertainment systems and refrigerators.

Next, Kircher acquired 22 companies in products ranging from audio equipment (KLH), home and office furniture, heating and air conditioning equipment, and so on. These, however, were relatively small companies, and Kircher was determined to acquire one more large company.

In 1968, General Precision (GP) was acquired for $450 million in stock. In addition to a profitable controls business, GP was involved in aerospace technology. Between 1963 and 1970, Kircher's objectives were frustrated by problems. Sales were up 160 percent to $2 billion, but earnings were up only 13 percent. The problems were many: operating setbacks, false starts, heavy debt, massive equity dilution, and an extremely high rate of executive turnover.

Friden was most troublesome. Sales declined, and profits of $8 million turned to losses. The problem was the mid-1960s electronics revolution of the business machine industry. Kircher had two choices when this revolution hit: (1) write off Friden, or (2) expand its small electronics operation. Since he had already invested so much, Kircher decided on the latter. Indeed, the decision to acquire General Precision was motivated in part by a desire to strengthen Friden in the electronics area.

In 1969, Friden's division manager, Alan Drew, was replaced by Robert Campbell, who had been in charge of General Precision's Link Division, which had been turned into a profitable line by Campbell. Kircher directed Campbell to put Friden into direct competition with IBM, Xerox, and NCR. He poured research and development money into the division and wanted new products: System 10, a satellite computer that competed with IBM's System 2, an office copier that was to compete with Xerox, and the Modular Data Transaction System (electronic cash register–point-of-sale equipment) to take NCR's traditional market. Kircher directed Campbell to introduce 15 new products in 15 months. After the failure of the office copier and a $3 million write-off, Kircher fired Campbell and replaced him with a former Burroughs executive.

There were other troubles. The product line extensions in the retail stores were not selling. Credit extensions in the Far East, Africa, and Latin America produced heavy write-offs. The mail-order business was not profitable. General Precision had many problems.

A major problem was still the high executive turnover. Out of 31 vice-presidents in 1969, only 16 were left by August 1971. Friden had three bosses in two years. The most notable departure was Alfred di Scipio, the apparent successor to Kircher after his success with the sewing machine business. One reason was di Scipio's opposition to the General Precision acquisition.

Kircher expressed confidence in his strategy and program in the early 1970s. Stockholders and directors were confident of Kircher's vision. He was still the golden boy.

Then, in 1974, Singer reported a loss of $10 million, its first since 1917 when it had to write off assets expropriated by the Russian Revolution. A basic source of the trouble was the company's $1.1 billion long-term debt. Fluctuating interest rates had created a serious debt-service burden. Another problem was internal wheelspinning. For example, $15 million spent by the industrial sewing machine division produced not one new product. The office equipment group was a continuing problem, posting enormous losses.

The board decided to act. Kircher was replaced in November 1975. Joseph Flavin was hired as Chief Executive and, in less than a month, made the decision to sell the business machine division and other money-losing acquisitions. In 1975, Singer reported sales of $2 billion and a loss of $452 million, one of the largest in corporate history.

KIRCHER'S PSYCHOLOGICAL TYPE

What went wrong? In order to get a perspective on how a brilliant and energetic man brought a company from stagnation and impending extinction to renewal and success and then again to the brink of disaster, I feel that we can gain deeper insights by examining Kircher's psychological makeup than by looking at so-called "objective" elements of his strategic failure. Jung's theory of psychological types provides, in my judgment, a real insight into both Kircher's strengths and weaknesses.

Kircher was, in my estimation, an extroverted, intuitive thinker. Let us examine these elements of his psychology in turn. His extroversion shows in his total fascination with objects. An example is his emphasis upon acquisitions, in spite of the many signals that he was becoming overextended. Kircher was absorbed by the object, and not only lost his company, but also himself in these objects. Jung says of the extrovert:

> for the tendency of this type is so outer-directed that even the most obvious of all subjective facts, the condition of his own body, receives scant attention. The body is not sufficiently objective of "outside" so that the satisfaction of elementary needs which are indispensable to physical well being is no longer given its due.[4]

This applies to Kircher, who, in his final days at Singer, had half of his stomach removed in a major surgical operation.

Kircher's perceptive function was clearly intuition. He was a man of vision. He saw the possibility of restoring Singer to greatness and perceived that greatness in the last half of this century would require restoring the strength and profitability of the basic sewing machine business. His vision also perceived the possibility of extending the product, volume, and profitability of this base by extending the product line in the Singer retail outlets, as well as the line of industrial machines. The final element of his vision was his belief in the possibility of establishing Singer in high-growth technology markets through acquisitions. This vision became a formula that was constantly invoked to suppress any opposition based on other ways of perceiving Singer's strengths and weaknesses, as well as on opportunities and threats in the business environment.

Kircher knew it all. He was perceived as brilliant by both the public and the board. He amazed his colleagues

[4]C. G. Jung, *Psychological Types*, paragraph 564.

with his uncanny ability to probe his executives with questions that got at the "heart" of situations, as well as with his ability to understand sophisticated technology and help to analytically solve problems. Kircher was able to do this from his highly analytical thinking orientation. While at Singer, Kircher developed an enormous library at home that allowed him to be well read in science, history, and biography. His lack of formal scientific training was made up for by his fascination with technology that he expressed by poring over textbooks.

According to Jung, the extroverted thinker "subordinates himself to his formula" and everyone "around him must obey it too, for whoever refuses to obey it is wrong—he is resisting the universal law, and is therefore unreasonable, immoral, and without a conscience."[5] Kircher's formula was his great desire to put Singer into growth markets outside the traditional sewing machine business. This was the theme of his leadership during his 18 years at Singer, and anybody who disagreed with him was fired or forced to resign. For example, when Alfred di Scipio, who successfully led the Consumer Products Group, opposed the General Precision acquisition, he was forced to resign. When anyone failed to accomplish the impossible, he was immediately replaced. This side of Kircher reflects his inferior, unconscious feeling. With no real feeling connection to his executives, he easily dismissed them when their "performance" fell short of objectives. This unconscious feeling, combined with inferior or unconscious sensation, ignored all facts: competition, obstacles, market position, time requirements for planning and implementation. Thus, Kircher was an autocrat ignoring valid facts and perceptions, blaming all failure on his own executives instead

[5]Ibid., paragraph 585.

of his own obtuse vision. His autocratic nature blocked his ability to hear his own management's opinions and perceptions, which were desperately needed if Singer was to proceed on a rational and realistic basis.

Kircher's powerful intellect and his ability to master facts easily swayed even his board of directors into unwise decisions. For example, his decision to acquire the housing subsidiary was opposed by a director knowledgeable in this field, but the director was unable to match Kircher's wit and rationale, and thus win over the other directors.

According to Jung, "The deeper we penetrate their [extroverted thinkers] own power province, the more we feel the unfavorable effects of their tyranny."[6] Kircher's tyranny took many forms. His deep devotion to Patton, his commander in World War II, led him to admire Patton's principle that in order to get his men to fight he must make them more scared of him than of the Germans. As a result, Kircher's management technique was, in his own words, the use of "fear."[7]

Since Kircher's superior functions were thinking and intuition, his inferior or unconscious functions were feeling and sensation. Instead of ensuring that he was covered in these areas, he simply ignored them. His inferior or unconscious feeling was shown by his ruthless treatment of executives. His rule of fear produced many new faces, but they were always inexperienced and never had time to develop and implement a strategy. Singer had a reputation as a revolving door and was, in its reign of terror, something very close to this.

The other area of Kircher's inferiority was sensation. His own executives and board counseled against many

[6]Ibid., paragraph 586.
[7]"How the Directors Kept Singer Stitched Together," p. 100.

of the acquisitions, but Kircher was blind to their perspectives. His formula would allow no other perceptions. A good example of how this operated was shown when J. C. Penney executives came to Singer to request POS terminals from Singer engineers. Before the meeting, Kircher reportedly told his engineers, "These people are going to tell us what they want, and they're damn well going to get it."[8] This kind of interference, which disregarded facts such as the relationship between cost and revenue, took its toll. Kircher's formula dictated that Friden would obtain the growth and profitability he desired: he willed this out of his grand design. The actual performance of Friden, however, was characterized by many observers as "unimaginative," and "Always a day late and a dollar short" in introducing new products.

The leadership style that expressed Kircher's one-sided thinking—intuitive orientation was autocratic. It owed its character to his repressed or inferior feeling, which made it impossible for him to have the trust and confidence necessary for delegation and real communication with his own executives. As a result, decisions were made by Kircher with little or no consultation. They were, as a consequence, decisions made without the benefit of relevant facts, but for Kircher the facts didn't really matter. Of course, if he were confronted with this appraisal, his extroverted side would deny any lack or regard for facts, but his own leadership and actions speak for themselves. Kircher's formula was elevated to the status of fact. The objective, in his mind, was a fact to be attained by the exercise of his own thinking and intuition.

---

[8]Ibid., p. 186.

Kircher's leadership of Singer is a very dramatic example of a man who considered himself to be bright enough to run a complex business all by himself. He never recognized his own weaknesses and limitations and could not value people who saw things differently. There is no question about Kircher's brilliance. Unfortunately, he allowed himself to be defeated by his own inferior or unconscious functions. Had he been aware of his weaknesses as well as his strengths, he would have valued and listened to executives who complemented his own strengths and weaknesses. The results would have been realistic goals and solid success instead of the Pyrrhic victory and Armageddon of his leadership.

As we have already pointed out, IBM is an example of a company that consciously values feelings.[9] This was particularly evident in the company under the leadership of Tom Watson, Sr. One of the very distinctive aspects of IBM in Watson's era was his belief that IBM was a family. In our extroverted, thinking culture, this was viewed as tremendous sentimentality. For example, Watson's devotion to family gatherings, which included not only executives and workers but also spouses and children, where the singing of IBM songs was a favorite diversion, was viewed by outsiders as a pathetic eccentricity and a laughable deviation from the U.S. cultural ideal, which celebrates the individual and regards any recognition of collective interdependence as a lapse in good taste.

At IBM, Watson's view of the company as a family was expressed in a number of significant ways. For example, under Watson's leadership, IBM had in effect a lifetime employment policy. IBM was a family and you do not fire

[9]Background on IBM is drawn from William Rodgers, *Think: A Biography of the Watsons and IBM* (New York: Stein and Day, 1969).

a family member. In a family, people are connected and this value permeated IBM. It is true that during Watson's era IBMers could be fired for a lack of sincerity, that is to say, a major deviation from Watson's other values such as the importance of white shirts, abstinence, particularly on the job, and other forms of what he considered disrespectful or outrageous behavior. However, if you were sincere, even incompetence was no ground for dismissal. You would not be promoted, but since the company was a family, you would not be fired. This policy created an atmosphere of security. Contrary to the assumption that holds that American workers and executives will never be committed to an organization, even in return for the organization's commitment to them, the commitment has been reciprocated by IBM workers and management.

Under Watson's leadership, IBM was an organization that drew with enormous effectiveness on the diverse talents of its management and employees. It is well known, for example, that IBM's entry into the computer business was an action carried out by his organization without his knowledge, which perceived the opportunity provided by computers and proceeded to take steps in research and development, which eventually placed IBM in a premier leadership position on one of the most dynamic markets of the last half of this century. I believe that the dedication and creativity of IBM's people is related directly to the quality of feeling, connection, and commitment, which Watson's orientation and leadership style created.

One of the best ways of developing the feeling function is to push yourself to discover your own values. Everyone has values, and everyone of course has feeling ability. The difference between people is the extent to which the feeling function is conscious and differentiated as opposed to unconscious and undifferentiated. Just as some people have developed and differentiated their thinking much more than others, so have some people developed and differentiated their feeling. The exercises which follow are designed to develop and differentiate your feeling function by pushing you to make yourself conscious of your own values.

FEELING EXERCISES

Exercise 1: Priorities

Life requires tradeoffs. We have only three score and fifteen years—and 24 hours in a day. You cannot do everything that you would like to do, you can only do what you do. What you do is a reflection of your values, and to a remarkable degree, unless you have really worked on finding out what your values are, what you do reflects unconscious values or ego choices of an ego that is not always entirely congruent with self or soul. This exercise is designed to help you determine what your priorities are.

Review each of the items on the following list, and give a numerical ranking to each item from 1 to 18. Force yourself to rank each item. When you have finished the ranking, do it again without looking at your first result. Then, put the exercise away for two weeks. After two weeks have elapsed, do the exercise again without looking at the results of your first pass. Note any changes that took place in your ranking during the two weeks. If your answers are stable, this is a possible indication that you really are clear on your priorities, at least for the moment. If your answers change, this is a good sign that your priorities are in flux, or that you are not yet clear on what they are.

SECURITY
CURRENT INCOME
FUTURE INCOME
PRESTIGE
FAMILY
CONTRIBUTION TO SOCIETY
HAPPINESS
HEALTH
LEISURE TIME
PROFESSIONAL GROWTH
PERSONAL GROWTH
LOVE
WORK
WEALTH
WORK PLACE ENVIRONMENT OR SETTING
GEOGRAPHICAL LOCATION
WORK RELATIONSHIPS AND INTERACTIONS—
FELLOW WORKERS/COLLEAGUES
FRIENDSHIP

Exercise 2: *Writing Your Own Eulogy*

Write your own eulogy. Imagine that you are sitting in the church, synagogue, temple, mosque, chapel, or auditorium. First, write the eulogy that you would like to hear. Be honest about the facts of your past, and be realistic about the possibilities in your future.

Next, write the eulogy that you would *not* like to hear. Again, be honest about the facts of your past, and be realistic about the possibilities. When you have completed Exercise 2, look at the results. What do your eulogies tell you about yourself? Are you doing what is really important to you? What do you really believe in? What are you really good at? What have you done that a eulogist might admire or take note of in remembering your life? Where have you made a contribution, and where do you feel you can make the greatest contribution at this point in your life?

Another approach to the question of discovering your own values is to reflect on your own eulogy. How would you like to be remembered? This is a way of getting at what is important to you. There are two phases to this exercise. The first is the determination of what is important to you now, as you look back over your life. After you complete this exercise, look at what you wrote. What did you remember? Is there a pattern in your selection? Is your eulogy consistent with your listing of priorities in Exercise 1? The second phase of this exercise is the determination of what it is you want to be remembered for during the remaining part of your life. This is the tough one. Here it will help if you ask yourself again, "What do I really believe in?" "What am I really good at?" "What kind of a contribution do I want to make to family, friends, and society?"

What is the eulogy that you would expect to hear if you continue on your present course? This is an excellent way of identifying what will happen in your life if you do nothing. This may be a satisfactory outcome, or there may be aspects that are unsatisfactory. Chances are, if it is satisfactory, it reflects the ordering of priorities you established in Exercise 1. If it is unsatisfactory, it more than likely does not reflect your Exercise 1 priorities.

The following exercise is designed to get you to focus on what you want out of life and where you are currently heading. If the two positions are congruent, no problem. If, however, there is a gap between what you want and your current direction, your work is cut out for you.

Exercise 3: What Do I Like to Do?

The purpose of this exercise is to give you a chance to assess what it is in life that gives you pleasure and satisfaction. Reflect over your life and write down what has given you the greatest pleasure and satisfaction during the past week.

During the past month?
During the past year?
During the past ten years?
During the past twenty years?
During your entire life?

Look at what you have written down. Where are your greatest pleasures? Are they changing as you grow older? If so, in what way?

Now, look ahead. What is it that would give you the greatest pleasure in the next month? Year? Five years? Ten years? Twenty years? Over the remainder of your life?

Exercise 4: What Am I Good At?

This exercise is designed to help you focus on things you do well. The emphasis now shifts from feelings to performance. Ideally, your feeling and your performance are aligned; that is, you like what you are good at. Notice, however, that I said "ideally." Now, it is time to be absolutely realistic about what, in fact, you are good at. Forget what you like and enjoy, and concentrate only on those things. Of course, "good" is a comparative term, so it is appropriate now to think about things you do well in comparison with others. Remember, it is absolutely essential to know what you are really good at because in life we are always competing with people who are leading from their strengths; we don't have a chance if we don't lead from our own strengths.

It may be helpful for you to reflect on your functions. Which function do you lead with? What is your strong suit? Chances are, what you are really good at comes relatively easily to you because it is your superior or most differentiated conscious function.

Another thought: don't limit your assessment to your working years. Unless you got into the right career, chances are there are some talents that you buried when you made your career choice. Reflect back to your childhood and school days. Again, at what things did you excel? How have you performed at your very best? In what ways are you outstanding?

Exercise 5: Gap Analysis

This exercise is designed to help you identify possible gaps between what you think are your priorities and what they actually are, and gaps between what you like to do and what you do well. One of the reasons you are not where you want to be is that you don't know who you are or where you want to be. If you did, you would be there. Therefore, gap analysis is a crucial step in sorting out the inconsistencies between your mind and your self.

Some readers may argue or take exception to this statement. You may be thinking, "Oh, I know where I want to be; my problem is that I can't get there." There is a mind trick. Your mind knows where it wants to be, but that is not the same thing as knowing where you want to be. Again, it is essential to know the differences between the mind, the self, the soul. The only thing that matters in the end is the soul or self. Where do you yourself truly want to be? This is the question. Once you have answered this question, you will know that you are on the path of what the Chinese call your Tao.

Look back now at your listing of priorities. Compare this listing with your eulogy. Do your priorities and your eulogy seem consistent? For example, if you wrote health down as your number one priority, do you exercise, refrain from smoking, and drink in moderation? If you listed family, has your life reflected this priority? If you listed current income, have you always put current income first in your tradeoff decisions or choices?

If your priorities and your eulogy are consistent, you are OK so far. If they are not consistent, then you have more work to do. What inconsistency tells you is that you are kidding yourself. Don't be discouraged if this is the case because it is true for 99 percent of the human race! If you find inconsistencies, keep working on your priorities and your eulogy. They should be consistent with each other.

The next stage of gap analysis is the comparison of what you like with what gives you pleasure, and with what you are good at. Drucker, as we have already mentioned, underlines the importance of knowing what you do well. This is performance. Here we are also interested in discovering what it is that you really care about. You are always going to be competing with people who enjoy their work. One of the reasons you will be competing with such people is that they are always the best in their field. People who enjoy what they do tend to be good at it. If there is a big gap between what you enjoy and what you are good at, then you need to find out how you got into this corner.

For example, assume that you put down that you enjoy theatre and movies, and that you truly appreciate a good performance by an actor. If you also put down that you are good at making presentations to audiences, perhaps one of your talents is acting. If your work gives you a chance to appear before audiences, perhaps you should recognize that inside you there is a desire or an appreciation of an actor's talent. You may find that by taking this more seriously you can integrate your pleasure and your work, and thus get more pleasure out of your work.

What if you put down that what you like is spending time alone in the forest? Does this mean that you should become a forest ranger? Not necessarily! Of course, you have to take into account all of your likes, preferences, needs, wants, and the alternatives open to you in life and find the best match. Many people make the mistake of quitting too early in this exercise and going for a job that is not really the right one in view of all of their talents and aptitudes. Remember that life is just one long list of tradeoffs. If you want to be a forest ranger, you face a very crowded field, limited possibilities for promotion and income, and difficulties in finding an entry-level job. Perhaps, in spite of everything, this is the right track for you, but perhaps not.

Exercise 6: Read Fiction and Poetry

One of the most enjoyable ways of getting in touch with your own feelings is through reading fiction and poetry. Indeed, the business of the novelist is to get readers in touch with feelings. Wright Morris, the American author, put this very well when he said, "I'm a writer and I'm just doing my business, the business of mingling emotion, memory and imagination to draw readers into feelings."[10] If you are a thinking type, chances are you will lean toward current events, business news, and nonfiction as opposed to fiction and poetry. If, in reviewing your reading habits, you conclude that you are not reading fiction and poetry, one of the ways to develop

---

[10]"Grateful Wright Morris Outgrows Regionalism," *The New York Times*, October 23, 1982, p. 12.

your feeling function is to change your reading habits. Put away the business press, or put limits on how much time you will devote to reading nonfiction, and budget some time for fiction. When was the last time you read a novel? A poem? If it was more than a month ago, stop and review your reading habits. You have a real opportunity to work on your feeling function and enjoy a good book, too.

LEADERSHIP

It is no secret today that the United States is losing in economic competition with the Japanese. Many Americans are puzzled by this. As a result, "microscopically examining Japanese management practices to discover the secrets of that nation's high productivity has become almost an obsession in U.S. business circles," say *Business Week* editors, who attribute the success to the existence of a quality of trust. "With all the savant's pronouncements on participatory management, one important element has been almost totally ignored. Japanese managers trust not only their workers but also their peers and superiors."[11]

Trust is a feeling quality, and it is not the only evidence of the extraordinary emphasis placed by Japanese executives on the quality of feeling. Life-long employment, employee participation in quality improvement, and long-range planning and programs are all characteristics of a management style that emphasizes feeling qualities of caring, respect, and sense of community, as well as mutual need and interdependence that charac-

[11]"Management Commentary," *Business Week*, July 6, 1981, pp. 104–105.

terize Japanese businesses. It is also perhaps significant, as noted before, that Japan is the largest offshore
user of the Myers-Briggs Type Indicator, a well known
Jungian type test: To date, over one million Japanese
workers have been tested as part of the intake process,
and retested again when confronting midlife career
changes.

The test has been administered by the Nippon Recruit
Center as part of a process that helps "match" employees and companies on the theory that a good fit between
the individual and the "atmosphere and climate" (an
interesting way to express it) is more important than a
good fit between training and tasks. Placement is often
made with a company "with no specific job immediately
in mind," according to the newsletter of the Association
for Psychological Types, an organization formed for the
users of the MBTI. Results of the MBTI and other tests
then become important to employers and new employees as they work out specific assignments within the
organization.[12]

Insight into the thinking of the Japanese executive
can be found in a series of monographs by Konosuke
Matsushita, founder and president of Matsushita Electric (National Panasonic), one of the world's most successful producers of electronic products. The essays are
a revealing glimpse into the Japanese mind offered by a
powerful and subtle thinker.

In the essay "The Untrapped Mind," Matsushita speaks
of the *sunao* spirit, which he describes as an "untrapped"
or open, unbiased, free mind, without "special bias,
emotionalism or preconceived ideas."[13] Now, in order to

---

[12]*MBTI News*, Newsletter of the Association for Psychological Types,
3(2), p. 1 (Spring 1981).
[13]Konosuke, Matsushita, "The Untrapped Mind," *PHP*, November
1980, pp. 88–91.

have an untrapped mind, a person must be able to separate perception and judgment, and be able to see things as they are, with differentiated sensation and intuition. It takes a lifetime to develop; this is not an overnight task. Similarly, with the differentiation of all the functions and typological development, we're talking about something that is not an instant gimmick or trick, but rather a model that can be a framework for developing an untrapped mind and for acquiring the spirit that will vary from one person to another. It is a fundamental spiritual attitude that an executive—or anyone—must have to be successful. It's an important task because without it one can neither enjoy genuine success in business (or anywhere else) nor enjoy genuine happiness in life. One of the things that Matsushita has done is to think about the purpose of an enterprise. His conclusion represents a very differentiated feeling conclusion, something that is still murky in America. He believes that the management of an enterprise or a company is essentially a public, not private, affair. All enterprises are tied to society, so they are public. You can't take a personal, selfish view, even in the management of a so-called "private" enterprise. All decisions must be made on the basis of what effect they are going to have on society. Thus, the whole question of responsibility is raised: how can fundamental corporate responsibilities contribute to the improvement of society through enterprise? At the same time, Matsushita believes that it is the duty of a company to earn a profit so that it can pay taxes and give a return to investors who have put society's resources at the management's disposal. This view places profit in perspective as a reflection or measure of the effectiveness in stewardship of society's resources. If there is a deficit, it proves that the organization is not performing its major responsibility, which is to contribute to society.

Matsushita also believes that the corporate executive should be concerned about the welfare of suppliers and dealers, and not negotiate terms that will harm them. Firm management policies should lead to coprosperity; this means that the executive must consider the other party's position and need to make a profit. Competition is necessary, but excessive competition can result in abusive management practices.

He also extolls the "public is always right" philosophy as an ordering principle in which the acceptance of society's collective values (an extroverted, feeling response) is a basis for orienting the enterprise. And, in relation to employees, Matsushita makes the point that management must explain the philosophy and policy of management to employees and respond to their questions. To be truly effective, he says, management must exist in the heart: this is the reason for management.

Now, all of this must seem utopian to the average "hard" American executive, who would probably regard it as "soft." The only problem is that the approach described by Matsushita works. His company is one of the leading firms of its kind in the world, and Japan is leading the race, not only in electronics but in automobiles, steel, and other products and commodities. The philosophy expressed is basically a feeling one.

In the contemporary American business culture, thinking is the dominant characteristic. In my testing, I have found that as many as 75 percent of the top level executives in American companies are thinkers. The high incidence of thinking types among successful executives in successful companies does not correspond with the frequency of thinking types in the general population, nor does it correspond with the requirements of the executive's job. It does not necessarily express the innate typology of contemporary executives. What it does express is a process of adaptation. Because our culture collectively favors the thinking function, executives and managers learn quickly to act, live, and manage through this function.

Unfortunately, the thinking leadership style is best suited to the individual whose superior function is thinking. For the executive whose superior function is feeling, it would be far better to employ a feeling leadership style, backed up with thinking. Similarly, for the person whose true function preference is thinking, back-up is necessary in the feeling function. For the intuitive, it will be needed in the sensation function, whereas for the sensation type, back-up is needed in the intuitive function.

Each of the four functions and both of the attitudes must be operating to enable an effective leader to deal with the complexities of the day-to-day requirements. This need for balance in the leader is in sharp contrast to the tendency to prefer and value one typology over another, and to reject and disparage those who are typologically different.

In the United States, the cultural bias in favor of thinking as opposed to feeling is quite evident in the pronouncements of many American chief executive officers when they emphasize that the primary goal of the organization is the profitability of "the bottom line." It is also apparent when executives talk of "being tough." Toughness is not strength; strength is the ability to consider all viewpoints without feeling threatened.

In "The Ten Toughest Bosses,"[14] *Fortune* Magazine profiles ten CEO's with reputations of being "toughest." Their common managerial philosophy might be summed

---

[14]Hugh D. Menzies, "The Ten Toughest Bosses," *Fortune*, April 21, 1980, p. 72.

up in the words of one chief executive: "Leadership is demonstrated when the ability to inflict pain is confirmed." Leaving out the question of a pathological sadism for the moment, one has to ask oneself if the so-called "toughness" is the reason for the executive's success—and not all of them are successful—or a secondary characteristic that may actually interfere with the brilliance most of these people display in their various management styles. Some of the consequences of this "infliction of pain" are illness and defection of staff (a wide variety of people were quoted—but not attributed—in the course of preparation of the *Fortune* article), and in several cases, a decrease in profitability from the constant turnover of executive talent.

Thinking is also apparent in organizations that pursue a plan or grand design without consulting and considering the opinions and feelings of the implementers, that is, the employees on whom everything depends. These attitudes and behaviors are symptoms of the emphasis on thinking. We hear them so much in American life that we assume they are expressions of eternal truths. They are not.

Another way of saying this is to recognize that today the business culture is rooted in the principle of *logos*, the Greek word for speech, word, and reason. The opposing principle to logos is *Eros*, the Greek god of love. *Eros* is, according to *Webster's Collegiate Dictionary*, the aggregate of pleasure-directed life instinct, whose energy is derived from the libido or psychic energy. To an American executive, it sounds preposterous to talk of this, but the fact is that the truly creative individual and organization is one that connects to creative energy and the *eros* principle. Without *eros* and feeling, we must rely on manipulation and raw power (hence the emphasis on being tough). Without *eros*, there can be no real pleasure in work and identification with the task for the worker.

In stark contrast to this stands the Japanese organization and the Japanese way. Japanese organizations are outperforming Western organizations today precisely because of the much greater cultural emphasis placed on *eros* and feeling as opposed to *logos* and thinking values. It would be unheard of, for example, for a Japanese chief executive officer to stand up before a group and baldly assert that the chief purpose of his company was the "bottom line." This would sound ridiculous to a Japanese audience, which feels, as we have shown, that the real purpose of an organization is to serve its *stakeholders* (employees, customers, and stockholders) and the public good. The major aim in Japanese companies is harmony and sincerity, both of which express *eros* and feeling values.

Eros is also the principle that binds people into a community—it is *eros* that creates a sense of identification with the organization's goals and programs, as well as an *esprit de corps* that encourages creative and committed effort. Feeling is the function of judgment that expresses the individual's values—what people care about. In order to connect with creative energy, an organization's leaders must be sensitive to the feeling values of its members.

The Japanese understand this and express it in their whole concept of leadership. The leader in a Japanese organization is really a facilitator. His or her function is to bring out the creativity of individuals and the group, rather than to act as the "wise one" or as the "hero" leading the way. The success of the Japanese business formula underlines the superiority of this approach.

It is significant that in World War II the external threat of an enemy forged a feeling commitment to the collective goal of survival and victory among Americans, both in service and in production. Today, another external threat is emerging. Today it is a major task of leadership in America to tap the energy and creativity of each individual and to integrate them into a coherent and effective expression. This can only be done if leaders are sensitive to individual needs and to the way people function.

Because of the confusion about the nature of feeling, it has the reputation of being "soft" and "mushy" in the American culture. Nothing could be further from the truth. Feeling can be decisive, and it certainly can be very hard, but it is never impersonal. The important thing about feeling in organizational life is that it must be recognized and valued in order to draw upon the creativity of the organization's leadership and members.

THE MAKING OF A LEADER

In his article, "A Style for All Seasons," Thomas J. Peters, formerly a principal of McKinsey & Company's San Francisco office, sums up the various characteristics of leadership. To someone who is familiar with the type theory, all of the qualities are represented. But there is a special emphasis on feeling. "The leaders we choose," says Peters, "are not simply those who present policies that make rational sense, they tend to be people who inspire confidence in us—confidence not based solely on reason."[15]

This ability to inspire confidence is based on the development of the feeling function; that is, the personal and instinctual qualities of the whole personality. One

[15]Thomas J. Peters, " A Style for All Seasons," *Executive*, April 21, 1980, pp. 12–16.

way of looking at feeling is to say it is expressed in the body as opposed to the head. Thinking, on the other hand, is in the head.

Obviously, thinking is necessary and valuable to a leader, but what really sets him or her apart is present in the body. Authority, the sense of conviction that the person really knows what he or she is talking about and really believes it, is a feeling quality. For example:

A marketing executive has made a terrific impact on his company, a giant corporation, by delivering messages on quality. He has talked to workers, he has done focus group interviews with customers, and he has learned that people care about quality. He is taking that message to the management of his company through memos, meetings, and presentations. He has done this successfully, with a quality of leadership based on a personal conviction that people do feel.

When you look at such leaders as General Eisenhower, Winston Churchill, and Charles DeGaulle, it is not necessary to take the position that they are feeling types; what is important is that they had this function available to them and they used it with thought, sensation, and intuition. The feeling function is felt with the entire body, and not just the head. This is the connection between leadership and type in that it points right to the development of feeling, which combines all of the other functions, intuition, sensation, and thinking, into a felt idea.

HIGH PERFORMANCE INDIVIDUALS

Studies of high performance or peak performance individuals suggest that they are different from average performers in terms of skills, how they work, how they manage stress, and how they approach risks. Charles A. Garfield, President of the Peak Performance Center in Berkeley and a clinical professor at the University of California at San Francisco Medical School, has studied peak performers for 15 years. After interviewing 1,200 peak performers in sports, business, the arts, education, and health care, he concluded that six characteristics mark optimal performers:

1. They are guided by internal goals and do what they do for the art of it.
2. They are able to transcend their previous levels of accomplishment.
3. They avoid the so-called comfort zones or plateaus of accomplishment that are comfortable.
4. They solve problems rather than place blame.
5. They take risks after laying out the worst consequences.
6. They mentally rehearse coming actions or events.

In addition to the six characteristics, Garfield found that these individuals are not Type A workaholics. They take vacations, know when to stop working, manage stress well, and don't get bogged down in details. They are, he says, masters of delegation.[16]

INTEGRATION: THE KEY TO ORGANIZATIONAL PERFORMANCE

Management must make decisions in the absence of total knowledge, under conditions of risk and uncer-

[16]"Why Do Some People Outperform Others: Psychiatrist Picks Out Six Characteristics," *The Wall Street Journal*, January 13, 1982, p. 33.

tainty. For this reason, management leadership requires feeling as well as thinking, sensation, and intuition to perform well. The general manager has to be the most rounded person on the team.

A manager plays many roles in the day-to-day tasks of managing. These roles include that of:

1. Figurehead
2. Leader
3. Liaison
4. Monitor
5. Disseminator (of information)
6. Spokesperson
7. Entrepreneur
8. Disturbance handler
9. Resource allocator
10. Negotiator

It is obvious that such a person must have highly developed capacities in each of the functions and must be able to value these qualities in others.[17]

The history of organizational life is a testimony to two realities: one is the folly of one-sided over-emphasis of one function or attitude over the other, and the other is the value and wisdom of complementarity in the organization. The wise leader appreciates that the superior organization will be based on planning, design, and rationality and, at the same time, on the recognition of the individual qualities of its managers. In such an organization, there is no one-sidedness. The futile debate over rationality versus human relations, or vice versa, is seen for what it is: a misunderstanding of the

[17]Henry Mintzberg, "The Manager's Job: Folklore and Fact," *Harvard Business Review*, July–August, 1975, pp. 49–61.

need for both kinds of attributes in an effective organization, and the incorporation of both of the functions these attributes represent. In this situation, the danger of becoming either inner or outer directed will be resolved in favor of healthy attention to the market and to the general opportunities and threats presented by the environment—as well as a sense of mission and organizational identity.

REFERENCES

Gaylin, Willard. *Feelings: Our Vital Signs.* New York: Harper & Row, 1979.

Gendlin, Eugene T. *Focusing.* New York: Everest House, 1978.

9

What Type Am I?
What Should I Do Now?

The conscious mind allows itself to be trained like a parrot, but the unconscious does not—which is why St. Augustine thanked God for not making him responsible for his dreams.

C. G. JUNG
(PSYCHOLOGY AND ALCHEMY)

INTRODUCTION

Many people know their type, if not by the terminology of the type model presented here, then certainly by their own understanding of their strengths and weaknesses. But knowing their own type is not such an easy thing for many other people. A surprising number are unaware of their actual type preferences. Introverts think they are extroverts; feelers think they are thinkers; and so on. Lack of self-knowledge can be costly. If we don't know our conscious or unconscious functions, we don't know our strengths and weaknesses. Knowledge of type can help us lead with our strengths and minimize the effects of our weaknesses.

Appendix 1 contains the Keegan Type Indicator, a pencil-and-paper instrument designed to allow you to determine your own type by answering and self-scoring 44 questions. Turn to this appendix now, answer the questions, and score your responses. The report of your function and attitude preferences is your type preference as suggested by the Indicator.

If your answers to the questions in the instrument produce a clear answer, and if you agree with that answer, chances are that this is your type. If your answers do not suggest a clear type preference, it may be because you are evenly developed typologically, or it could mean that you have not differentiated any of your functions and they are all in a state of relative underdevelopment. If the latter is the case, you have not developed your superior function, which should be your leading tool for adapting to life.

Appendix 2 is an exercise you can try if you are part of a group that has completed the Keegan Type Indicator or another type test or indicator. It is a storywriting and group report assignment. The first part of the assignment is the individual story describing your conception of the ideal organization. After writing your individual story, you join a group of type-similar people and prepare a group report on the ideal organization. I have conducted this exercise dozens of times with groups of managers in the United States and in Europe. They have never ceased to be amazed at the differences between the group conceptions of an ideal organization. What this exercise demonstrates is that different types have very different conceptions about what an ideal organization would look and feel like, and about its focus. Most managers concluded, at the end of this exercise, that the really ideal organization would have a good mixture of each of the types in its membership.

HOW DO I COMPARE WITH OTHERS?

Table 9.1 is a summary of empirical studies of the frequency of types. The best estimate of the population at large in the United States is the CAPT data bank of 75,745 cases collected between 1970 and 1976, primarily by secondary and college counseling offices. This data suggest that people are relatively evenly distributed between extroverts and introverts, and between thinking and feeling types. The relatively low frequency of superior sensation as compared to superior intuition (16 percent vs. 30 percent) is surprising. It may reflect a bias in the sample or in the MBTI instrument, rather than an actual distribution in the population. It may also express a bias in the culture. In any event, when a test or a self-report indicates that a person prefers one function over the other, this does not necessarily mean that the person prefers his or her own superior function. It could just as well mean that the person is in a type falsification situation.

What stands out in Table 9.1 is the contract between the managers of a large, multinational U.S. corporation, as compared to the CAPT data bank and the MBA students at the Wharton School and George Washington University. Seventy-five percent of the senior functionate managers and 68 percent of the division managers in this company are thinkers, as compared to 24 percent of the national sample, 32 percent of the George

Table 9.1 Frequency of Types

	Center for Application of Psychological Types Data Bank[1]	Wharton Business School Students[2]	George Washington University M.B.A. Candidates[3]	Division Managers of a Large U.S. Multinational Corporation[4]	Senior Functional Managers of a Large U.S. Multinational Corporation[5]
Extroverts	53%	70%	64%	55	
Introverts	47	30	36	45	
Superior Intuition	30	19	23	16	8
Superior Sensation	16	28	16	3	8
Superior Thinking	24	38	32	68	75
Superior Feeling	30	15	29	13	10

[1] 75,745 cases collected between 1970 and 1976. Source: MBTI News, Vol. 1, No. 1, 1976. Center for Application of Psychological Types, 1976.

[2] 488 cases. Source: Myers, Isabel Briggs, the Myers-Briggs Type Indicator Manual, Palo Alto, California: Consulting Psychologists Press, 1962.

[3] 69 cases, February 1978. Degree Candidates in Business Policy Course. Source: Myers-Briggs Type Indicator.

[4] 31 cases, February 1978. Source: Myers-Briggs Type Indicator.

[5] 112 cases, 1978. Source: Myers-Briggs Type Indicator.

Washington University M.B.A. candidates, and 38 percent of the Wharton School students.

These findings raise a number of questions: Why is there such a great preference for thinking in the large, multinational corporation as compared to the CAPT data bank and the business students? There are a number of possible explanations, but it appears very likely that the company sample is a reflection of the company management style, which is very heavily oriented toward planning and finance. In order to succeed in this company, employees must adopt the prevailing management style. Is such a predominance of thinkers or the thinking style good or bad? In itself, it is neither good nor bad. It becomes good or bad only if the style is so predominant that it suppresses the ability of management to perceive reality and if it suppresses needed sensitivity to feelings of organization members.

Two questions are raised by the knowledge of type for the individual: First, "Does my life provide the necessary scope or the opportunity to use my primary function?" If not, mediocrity will be forced upon the individual because nothing but a highly differentiated function, engaged in work that gives it the scope to compete with other highly differentiated functions, can compete in this world. Success goes only to the primary function that has found the right job. *Period.*

The second question raised is: "Are my two intermediate or the second and third functions sufficiently differentiated to support my primary function?" There must be a balance between perception and judgment, and between extroversion and introversion. Extreme extroversion is always superficial, and extreme introversion is always unpractical.

WHAT SHOULD I DO?

Peter Drucker has three questions for people who ask him for career advice:

1. What are you really good at?
2. What do you really believe in?
3. Where could you make a contribution that really makes a difference?

Notice that Drucker does not ask, "What do you like?" He believes that it is much more important to establish what you are good at, and that your actual past performance is a more reliable guide to your strengths than are your likes and dislikes.

But, you may say, doesn't everyone agree that in order to be really good at anything one must like what one is doing? Emerson himself said, "Nothing great was ever achieved without enthusiasm." Shouldn't we begin the process of self-assessment by finding out what we like and then proceed to do that?

The fact of the matter is that Drucker has a very good point. We are all incredibly good at lying to ourselves. We say we like something and, in fact, the opposite may be true. One of the most important exercises in life assessment and career planning is the serious work required to establish what it is that we like.

The problem with going directly to the question of "What do I like?" is that the mind lies. The mind is good at coming up with extroverted answers to the question. All of us at one time or another have been influenced by parents, teachers, and cultural values, and to an amazing degree, our likes are simply what we have picked up from others. The fact that we have picked up these "likes" means that they are somewhere in us, but this is far from a truly differentiated, conscious feeling.

The word "*likes*" in quotes refers to what our minds think we want or like. The word without quotes refers to actual personal likes or differentiated feeling. True likes must come out of the self, or the core of our individuality.

MIND VERSUS SELF

The mind is extroverted ego, and the self is introverted soul. In a typical person, the ego and self are partially overlapping and partially in conflict. Whenever there is a discrepancy between self and ego there are problems. This is a source of suffering, and the only way out of this suffering is to face the problem and work on finding out about yourself.

One of the ways of finding out what you like is to address your priorities. One of the most fundamental facts of life is that we must choose. The myth of childhood, the illusion of youth, is that we can have it all. When we are young we believe in omnipotence: eternal life, fame, love, glory, power, friendship, family, security, money. Life represents tradeoffs, and the only way to rationally approach the question of tradeoffs is to address your own introverted feeling. What are your values? What is important to you?

CAUTION: DON'T "TYPE" PEOPLE

One of the greatest dangers of any type theory is the almost compelling tendency to "type" people. This is pointless and futile in view of the enormously complex and varied aspects of the human personality. As we have said, there are, in the English language, almost 10,000 words that describe aspects of personality. To the extent that language is a mirror of reality, this enormous variety of words gives some idea of the complexity we are dealing with. Obviously, a mere 16 "types" is no way to completely explain the enormous variety of human personalities.

The value of the type theory is that it provides a framework for the understanding of how we perceive reality and how we arrive at judgments. Much apparently random variation in human behavior is actually an orderly and consistent expression of preferences for perceiving and judging.

We must understand that misused type generalizations can blind us to the specific and the particular. It is a valuable insight to know that a person relies on thinking or feeling, for example. But this tells us nothing about how individuals think or feel, whether they have highly developed thinking or differentiated, conscious feeling, or whether they are good or bad. In short, it does not tell us much about the personality or the individuality of a human being.

PROBLEM-SOLVING STYLES

Typology can be related to problem-solving in a way that can help an individual identify the best probable choice of career. If we know how our mind works to solve problems, we can begin to understand what type of career we are most likely to succeed at. Society and the business world have tended to favor one style of problem-solving—systematic thinking—over the intuitive approach, valuing the first as logical and organized, while branding the second as chaotic and disorganized. What is not understood is the *method* the intuitive problem-solver uses, because it is hidden from everyone, often even the intuitive himself. Despite this, two professors claim that the intuitive approach is just as effective as the systematic style. According to James L. McKenney of Harvard Business School and Peter G. W. Keen of the Stanford Business School, who have studied nearly 200 graduate business students, "each has unique advantages and . . . neither can be called superior to the other."[1]

They found that "the intuitive mode is not sloppy or loose . . . it seems to have an underlying discipline at least as coherent as the systematic mode." Describing the frequent scorn heaped on intuitives by sensation and thinking types who can plan their strategies and then delegate parts of the action, they point out that intuitives are more likely to excel if the problem is elusive and difficult to define. They keep coming up with different possibilities, follow their hunches, and don't commit themselves too soon, redefining the problem as they go along.

The discipline of developmental psychology divides problem-solving into a two-step process: gathering information and using it. McKenney and Keen hypothesize that intuitives begin with an "image" of the problem, while thinkers concentrate on details and build up a premise. Various problems were then offered to the student group under study. The two then began to realize that, in addition to these two basic ways of approaching problems, people fall into two groups in the ways that they gather information. They call them "preceptive" and "receptive" information gatherers. Preceptive types begin with a system of how to deal with the information

[1]David W. Ewing, "Discovering Your Problem-Solving Style," *Psychology Today*, December 1977, pp. 69–70; 73; 138.

according to a "preconceived" mental concept. "They pay close attention to relationships between facts."[2]

Receptive types take in details and assimilate facts without an organizing principle. "They are fascinated with the 'feel' and inherent qualities of new facts, rather than their possible relationship to other facts. They suspend judgment and avoid preconceptions," say McKenney and Keen, who cite Sherlock Holmes as an example of this type.

> Holmes is always at odds with the preceptive styles of Dr. Watson and the detectives of Scotland Yard, who zero in on the 'obvious' suspect and fit the facts to build a case against him. Holmes is titillated by odd and assorted facts, and on the basis of trifling details uncovers more leads and finally builds a hypothesis that leads to the murderer.[3]

Other terms for this cognitive process are inductive thinking, leading away from the fact to a conclusion about the whole or deduction, reaching a conclusion that is built up by a selection of facts.

Both intuitives and (systematic) thinkers use either style of information gathering, say McKenney and Keen. Thus, they identify four cognitive styles:

1. Systematic thinkers
2. Intuitive thinkers
3. Receptive thinkers
4. Preceptive thinkers

About three-fourths of the people studied fell into

[2]Ibid., p. 70.
[3]Ibid., p. 70.

one category or another. The remainder favored one style but did not use it exclusively.

Understanding oneself and one's preferred cognitive method is essential in making a career choice. The results of McKenney and Keen's studies, which tracked 82 graduates, showed "clear differences between systematic thinkers, who tended to choose careers in production, planning, control, and supervision in industry and the military, and the intuitive thinkers, who preferred careers in psychology, advertising, library science, teaching, and the arts."[4]

PITFALLS OF PROMOTION

Just as an individual can mature into his or her career or destiny, one can fail to mature enough to keep pace with a developing career. Everyone knows the brilliant engineer who was promoted to vice-president of engineering and lived to regret it. People achieve success in life largely on the basis of their conscious or differentiated function. The one-sided development, which may have served them well in the early stages of their career, can become a cause of failure if they are subsequently promoted to positions requiring the use of functions that are unconscious, undeveloped, or undifferentiated in their youth and that do not emerge during their growth toward maturity.

Example: A successful salesman, whose high earnings are based on highly differentiated sensation, is promoted to vice-president of sales. The new position requires not only sensation, the ability to sense and react to what is

[4]Ibid., p. 73

immediately happening, but also creative intuition in order to develop long-range plans. It is not required that our exsalesman suddenly become an intuitive type; he can't. As we have shown, type is innate. One cannot change type anymore than the leopard can change spots. What this new vice-president must do, however, is recognize that intuition must be expressed within his organization or his department will fail. He must, at the same time, begin to get in touch with his own largely unconscious intuition so that it is available when he requires it.

The same pitfall occurs in reverse when the intuitive, creative marketing executive is promoted to top management. In this new leadership role, imagination and creativity are not enough; the manager must also be able to ensure that the business does not get out of control as he or she chases the endless new possibilities that a creative imagination suggests and that may have won the promotion. This intuitive must recognize and value the sensation function in others so that the organization can benefit from a total performance of all the available functions through a well-balanced staff.

CONFRONTING THE UNCONSCIOUS FUNCTION

One of the greatest benefits of type self-knowledge is the insight it provides into our own weaknesses. Only when we have identified our unconscious functions can we consciously act to call them forth when they are required. In order to do this, we must consciously suppress the opposite, or conscious, function. The intuitive must consciously suppress intuition of possibilities in a situation in order to concentrate on what is actually going on at the moment. The sensation type must let go of perception of the immediate situation to reflect on the possibilities not expressed in sense-perceived facts. Similarly, the thinker whose life is ordered by logical and impersonal thought must consciously suppress this function to focus on the values concerning the matter at hand. The feeler, by contrast, needs to suspend the tendency to particularize and individualize response to a situation by backing off and addressing questions of logical consistency and sound structure.

Example: In a problem in organizational design, the thinker is prone to ignore individual and personal qualities, motivations, and capabilities and design the "ideal" structure. The end product may be theoretically sound, but it will fail to respond to the human capabilities of the people who will be required to work within an "ideal," and hence unreal, design.

The opposite occurs when organizations are designed only on the basis of individual capabilities that ignore organizational logic and theory. In these cases, the design starts out based on individual strengths and weaknesses, then becomes riddled with internal inconsistencies and a general lack of logical organization and focus. What begins as an organization designed for people becomes an organization that defeats them.

The same approach distinguishes the individual seeking to maximize the unconscious function. For the intuitive, a good way to go is to suspend for a while the pleasure of thinking about possibilities and engage in some sensation-type activities, such as straightening out the office. For a sensation type, one way to develop intuition is through group exercises, such as those developed by organizations like Synetics in Cambridge.

These exercises use methods like brainstorming, in which people are asked to speculate about solutions to a problem with a total suspension of judgment. In other words, nobody is allowed to criticize or judge the sometimes wild ideas that emerge. In a warm and supportive atmosphere, one can release creativity and intuition— and sometimes surprising things can result.

Regarding some of the training conducted by typologically oriented management training experts, it is worthwhile to refer again to Dean Holt's comments about his management training workshop. In Chapter 6, Holt is experienced enough to be suspicious of instant feedback from his workshop sessions. He contacts people four months later to inquire about their retention and use of the MBTI testing and the Jungian typology concepts to which they were exposed. "Although," he says, "the sample is by no means large enough to justify generalizations, those I talked with remembered the concepts, most of the language of the concepts, and how to use their newly acquired knowledge on the job." There are three main areas where the training made a recognizable difference for them: (1) personnel evaluations, (2) building support systems for self in the manager role, and (3) selecting staff members according to the nature of the task. One manager reported that he perceives and understands others much more accurately, is able to spot "functional type episodes," if not whole psychological types, and is able to respond more appropriately to the situation as a result—that is, "in general, to be able to respond more fully and completely to reality."

MANAGEMENT IN THE AGE OF AQUARIUS

The shocking drop in productivity in the United States (from first in the world in the post—World War II decade

to seventh in the 1980s), is forcing some hard reapprais-
als of our approach to business management and the
way in which people are—and are not—utilized in industry. There is no question that we are trying to fit
everybody into an increasingly narrow and rigid idea of
what makes a good executive. The rising tide of dissatis-
faction and failure is underscored by Fernando Bartolome and Paul A. Lee Evans, whose article in the *Harvard
Business Review*, "Must Success Cost So Much?," points
out the problems. In addition to the personal misery of
the misfit between job and person, "spill-over tension"
can destroy not only careers but marriages, as they
graphically point out.[5]

Stung by the outstanding success of other industri-
alized countries in integrating the personal needs of
people with the demands of production, American corporations today are looking at their recruiting and
training procedures anew. Perhaps never before in history has so much money, time, and attention been paid
to the human psyche. However, so far the use of psychology, human potential concepts, and various behavioral
theories have all failed to create a working environment
in the United States in which people can be productive
and happy at the same time.

Richard Pascale, of Stanford University, is not one of
those who laud the Japanese style over that of American
managers. He finds that "When technology and government factors are equal, the Japanese companies' U.S.
subsidiaries do not outperform their American coun-
terparts.[6] According to Pascale, both Japanese and

[5]Fernando Bartolome and Paul A. Lee Evans, "Must Success Cost So
Much?" *Harvard Business Review*, March–April 1980, pp. 137–
148.
[6]Richard Tanner Pascale, "Zen and the Art of Management," *Harvard Business Review*, March–April 1978, pp. 153–162.

American managers are skilled in the subtle use of participative management techniques and the ability to achieve effective organizational functioning. He does, however, feel that an understanding of the Japanese or Eastern concept of Zen (meditation) is helpful in understanding how both groups achieve their success:

> Actually, I discovered only two significant differences between Japanese and American companies: (1) Three times as much communication was initiated at lower levels of management in the Japanese companies. . . . (2) While managers of Japanese companies rated the quality of their decision-making the same as did their American counterparts, they perceived the quality of implementation of those decisions to be better.[7]

He found that the successful managers of both nationalities tended to "guide" subordinates to their point of view, without disclosing it beforehand, through the use of questions. Sometimes the subordinates' reactions would change the *a priori* opinion of the manager. "The more significant finding is that successful managers *regardless of nationality* share certain common characteristics that are related to subtleties of the communications process."[8]

Pascale calls Zen a "description of an implicit" rather than explicit dimension, and explains that while both Japanese and Americans (and others) use it, it is more an outgrowth of Eastern "philosophy, culture and value" than it is of the West, and Americans "must swim upstream culturally" to achieve results. He finds positive qualities to be found in ambiguity—having a dual frame of reference that recognizes both the clear and the am-

[7]Ibid., p. 154.
[8]Ibid., p. 156.

biguous instead of the relentless clarity valued by Western culture. Ambiguity, for example, can be useful when an executive has enough or even too much data to make a decision but is aware that the decision might affect human feelings and behavior. Thus, by using ambiguity, he uses the data to decide to proceed—allowing room for others to react before proceeding.

> Ambiguity has two important connotations for management. First it is a useful concept in thinking about how we deal with others, orally and in writing. Second it provides a way of legitimizing the loose rein that a manager permits in certain organizational situations where agreement needs time to evolve or where further insight is needed before conclusive action can be taken.[9]

Managers use ambiguity to approach a subordinate without crowding him or her. This approach makes use of the qualities of intuition and feeling: intuition, or in this case empathy, in order to anticipate the subordinate's responses, and feeling, in order to perceive them as they happen. People's feelings are hurt when they are told flatly that they are wrong. Yet Western culture puts a high premium on such bluntness and the ability to take it. The Eastern equivalent of "face" or pride exists just as concretely in the American psyche, but we regard it as a weakness instead of a basic part of human nature. However, business losses resulting from attempts by humiliated workers to get even are forcing American managers to reconsider the value of a tough stance. Pascale says that, "The evidence suggests that explicitly crowding a person into a corner may, in many instances, be not only unwarranted but also counterproductive. If

[9]Ibid., p. 62.

you have to work with that person on a continuing basis, macho confrontations complicate life immensely."

Another attribute of a Zen or feeling approach is recognition. In an AMA survey cited by Pascale,[10] 49 percent of the respondents indicated that recognition for what they did was their most important reward. "Recognition," he says, "may become an increasingly important 'fringe benefit' since a central problem facing American society is how to reward people in a period of slowed growth when employees win promotions and raises less often." He comments on people's lack of response when they are asked to contribute or change but are denied recognition. "It's an ironic axiom of organization that, if you are willing to give up recognition, in return you gain increased power to bring about effective change." Pascale points out the value of "implied recognition," where a person's qualities are recognized by having his or her opinion solicited. An invitation to a significant meeting "from which the person might otherwise have been excluded," is always an offering of implied recognition.

"Eastern perspective provides a further insight," says Pascale.

> It reminds us that the real organization you are working for is the organization called yourself. . . . The sense of the implied for accommodation and timing and the sense of the expressed for the jugular must be woven together like strands in a braided rope, alternatively appearing and disappearing from sight but part of the whole. . . . Good executives master the art and the science of management—not just one or the other.[11]

---

[10]G. McLean Preston and Katherine Jillson, "The Manager and Self Respect," *AIA Survey Report*, New York: AMACOM, 1975.
[11]Pascale, "Zen and the Art of Management," p. 159.

Many Western executives show concern for their subordinates, and these people with good interpersonal skills are highly valued. "Good managers," Jay Hall has said, "use an integrative style of management in which production goals and people's needs are equally important."

Pascale does comment on the loneliness of the American workers, in thrall to the dehumanized, systematized, Western concept of organization. To the Japanese, organization relates to the system of management; they think of the company in which the worker is absorbed as a whole human being with "a shared sense of values." "The company . . . reflects a commitment to larger ends than just the accomplishment of a mission," says Pascale.

Japanese firms meet the needs of their workers to be rewarded (e.g., paid), to be accepted as unique, and to be appreciated "not only for the function performed but also as a human being." They spend, on an average, more than three times as much per employee on social and recreational facilities than do American firms, and provide opportunities for twice as much contact between workers and supervisors. The results have no impact on the bottom line. However, to the Japanese, the "bottom line misses the point." He says, "To the Eastern mind it is 'man,' not the 'bottom line,' that is the ultimate measure of all things." The Japanese, Pascale states,

> proceeds with a dual awareness—that there is a second ledger in which 'success' is debited or credited in terms of his contribution to the quality of relationships that ensue. So the professional manager defines his role not only as one who accomplishes certain organizational tasks but also as an essential intermediary in the social fabric.[12]

[12]Ibid.

This attitude represents a feeling quality.

Jung's typology is among those theories that are gaining ground in education and in management training, as people begin to see that it offers an objective, nonjudgmental way to view the workings of the human mind. If the system were to be more widely used and incorporated into regular intake procedures, it would give a company an objective look at the human potential within its grasp, and a way of avoiding the square-peg-in-a-round-hole syndrome.

At the same time, if corporate executives had a knowledge of typology and used it to develop their teams and task forces; to evaluate staff in terms of task; to develop an objective way to review differences of opinion in the conference; and to understand themselves, their performance, and that of their companies, they would improve immeasurably without the conflict and rancor that characterize so much corporate behavior today.

More, of course, is needed. The vaunted American tradition of "hard-nosed thinking" has to open up to permit the other functions to operate. Only then, with a full complement of the available talent, can we begin to solve the problems of the 1980s and create a rational future for American business and society at large.

10

Summing Up: Implications for Management

To be what we are, and to become what we are capable of becoming, is the only end of life.

R. L. STEVENSON

Jung's type theory is a management tool of enormous potential. The four functions are the psychic or mental basis for all management action. The 16 combinations of attitude and function result in personalities with different strengths and weaknesses, and distinctly different orientations to perception and decision-making. In the section that follows, the major implications of Jung's theory for management are outlined.

THE IMPORTANCE OF SELF-KNOWLEDGE

To recognize the typological character of others, we must first of all be able to identify our own typology. In my work with executives, I find a surprising number who are unaware of their actual typology. Introverts think they are extroverts, feelers think they are thinkers, and so on. This gap in self-knowledge can be very dangerous and costly. If we are unaware of our superior and inferior functions, we are unaware of our greatest strengths and our most serious areas of weakness. Knowledge of our psychological type can help us to trust our superior function, and even more importantly, it tells us where we need to seek help and work the hardest.

CAVEATS AND LIMITATIONS

One of the greatest dangers of Jung's type theory is the almost compelling tendency to use the theory to "type" people. This is a pointless and futile effort in view of the enormously complex and varied aspects of human personality. Several years ago, investigators identified almost 18,000 words in the English language which described aspects of personality. To the extent that language is a mirror of reality, this enormous variety of words gives some idea of the complexity of personality. Obviously, a theory with a mere 16 types falls far short of the variety of human personality.

The purpose of the type theory is rather to provide a theoretical framework that gives insight into how the mind or psyche functions. As such, it is a great help in expanding our understanding of how we, ourselves, and others perceive the world and make decisions. Much apparently random variation in human behavior is actually orderly and consistent expression of preferences for ways of using perception and judgment.

Nevertheless, we should always keep in mind that, if misused, the type polarities can blind us to the specific and the particular. It is a valuable insight to know that a person relies on thinking or feeling, for example. But nevertheless, this does not tell us about how this person thinks or feels, or whether the person has highly developed thinking or highly developed, articulated, and differentiated feeling.

Jung himself realized this, and in a revision of *Psychological Types* emphasized that it was not the purpose of the theory to type people into categories. He referred to this form of typing as a childish parlor game. The purpose, he emphasized and underlined, was to provide a critical psychology and a framework for a more differentiated understanding of how people perceive and judge.

FALSIFICATION OR REVERSAL OF TYPE

Is our psychological typology inherited or learned? It appears that type characteristics are inherited or genetically imprinted. This conclusion is based on the frequent occurrence of different typology in identical twins who are raised in the same home, and on the observation of children who, very early in life, exhibit type characteristics that are different than those of their parents. Indeed, there appears to be a rather widespread incidence of what could be described as falsification of type or reversal of type. These cases occur when a child is raised by parents in a milieu insensitive to the child's character, and when the child responds by adopting both attitudes and/or preferences other than his or her innate function or preference. For example, a child might be an intuitive feeler born into a family with a tradition of academic achievement. Such a child could be encouraged to excel academically as a thinker to the point of forging his or her adaptation to life on the basis of the thinking function. This, of course, would be enormously supported and encouraged by the wider culture, especially for male children. Since thinking and feeling are opposed, this falsification or reversal results in the suppression of the innate superior or preferred function. This may work, and even work rather well in the first half of life, but as a person gets older, alienation from the innate or preferred function will lead to increasing feelings of inner conflict, tension, and neurosis. I once knew a man who was born an intuitive feeler but whose parents expected him to win the Nobel Prize. As expected, he majored in science and as a very young man achieved academic accolades. However, his scientific accomplishments were always modest and were always obtained at a very high cost to his own personal sense of well-being and happiness. Later in life, this man was fortunately able to get in touch with his preferred function and admit to himself that he was not, indeed, a Nobel scientist, but rather a very effective and skillful academic administrator. Today he is a very happy and successful university department chairman. Before, he was an extremely frustrated researcher who always felt like a total failure in his field.

To recap from Chapter 2, there are three stages of the development of type in an individual's life. The first is the initial stage, when the dominant or preferred functions and attitude of the child are recognizable to the sensitive and perceptive adult. This is a crucial stage in the development of the child, and one in which sensitivity to individual character can have a profound significance in the child's future development.

The second stage of type development is in young adulthood to middle life, when the individual controls and suppresses one or more functions in order to achieve success and adaptation academically and in careers. In our sensate, thinking culture, this often involves the suppression of intuition and feeling in order to achieve academic and business success. For the more fortunate young adults, academic and career choices are matched to functional and attitude preference.

The third stage of type development is when the individual reaches mid-life and begins to give more attention and recognition to functions that have been suppressed or relatively undervalued. This can be a very turbulent stage in life. For example, conflict in marriage may develop when each partner seeks to exercise functions that have been left to the other. It is also a time of career change, with many people seeking a second career or redefining their objectives and goals to reflect their total personality, including functions which may not have been adequately valued and expressed in the first half of life.

THE PITFALLS OF TYPE SIMILARITY

One of the dangers of unconscious psychological typology is the tendency to prefer association with similar types at work. People of our own type perceive and decide on the same basis as we do, and are therefore compatible. The problem with this is that when we associate with our own type, we cut ourselves off from the opposite and equally valid ways of perceiving and deciding.

For example, the president of a leading company in the packaging industry is an intuitive, thinking type. He had perceived the possibilities of a new industry technology at the beginning, and had achieved in 15 years a dominant position in the new and fast-growing segment of the industry by concentrating on "creativity," expressed largely in the form of new applications for his company's packaging system. The industry had matured, and competition was increasingly based on price as opposed to the ability to work with customers or application problems. In emphasizing creativity, the president overlooked the finer points of cost control: for example, his company operated regional plants, but had not standardized cost accounting or functional manufacturing management. Each plant manager was idealized as an entrepreneur.

Unconsciously, the president realized that he needed to concentrate on cost management in order to maintain his position as industry leader. Consciously, he continued to operate with his superior function. He talked about creativity, about having fun, of course! To an intuitive, nothing is more depressing than concentrating on details and minding the store. The intuitive is always looking around the corner for new possibilities.

What the president needed was a person of opposite superior function: a sensate who would delight at the opportunity to move into the company and install a standard cost accounting system and work on achieving the lowest possible costs in the industry. Instead, he hired a bright young intuitive M.B.A. who wrote magnificent memos outlining the magnificent possibilities for diversification into new fields! He was another intuitive thinker. The president and his new assistant were very compatible, but the company desperately needed the talents of a man who could manage a cost-management program and focus the company on the goals of achieving cost superiority over competition: in other words, a sensate.

COMPLEMENTARITY OF OPPOSITE TYPES

The clearest vision of the future comes from an intuitive, but the most practical realism comes from the sensing type. The most incisive analysis is the strength of a thinker, and the most skillful handling of people and relating of different kinds of talents are the strengths of a feeling type. Success for any enterprise demands a variety of types, each in the right place, focused on an appropriate task.

Opposite types supplement each other in joint endeavors. When two people approach a problem from opposite sides, each sees things that are not visible to the other. Unfortunately, since they do not see things from each other's point of view, it is difficult for people of complementary types to work well together. Probably the best teamwork is accomplished by people who differ on only one or two of the type aspects. This much difference is useful, and the two or three aspects they have in common provide a bridge that aids understanding and communication.

It is essential, when opposite types live or work together, that they understand the characteristics of type differences in perceiving and decision-making. Different perceptions of different ways of deciding are much less irritating when people understand the origin of the differences. Instead of finding the other person willfully contrary and obstreperous, he can be recognized as an opposite but complementary type who is tremendously useful in illuminating reality and the grounds and basis for a decision.

Recognizing the value and validity of different ways of perceiving and decision-making in complementary types is an invaluable managerial insight. Too often, however, when we find someone who is not like us, we reject him or her as being stupid or inferior. This unfortunate tendency, if not checked, can lead to organization staffing that is unconsciously seeking type similarity rather than type complementarity.

One of the reasons that business schools are often

such depressing places to intuitive and feeling types is that the business school places its greatest value on thinking and sensation while repressing intuition and feeling. As a consequence, the thinking in a business school setting often becomes depressingly sterile. There is not enough value placed on the other functions. It is the familiar phenomena of like-minded people gathering together, reinforcing their own prejudices and suppressing the potential creativity, that can come out of a more diverse group. This is particularly unfortunate in a school if it results in the suppression of intuition, the sixth sense that perceives possibilities not inherent as "facts" perceived by the five senses.

Table 10.1 summarizes the ways in which different types complement each other.

COMPLEMENTARITY IN MANAGEMENT:
THE AMDAHL CORPORATION EXAMPLE

In 1970, Gene M. Amdahl, computer designer and architect of IBM's Series 360, quit IBM for the second time. In a bluntly worded letter of resignation, he declared his intention of competing with IBM by producing large-scale computers that would run on IBM software. In 1976, the first full year of Amdahl Corporation's operations, the company reported profits at $24 million on revenues of $93 million.[1]

Two key individuals have been involved in the leadership of Amdahl Corporation. The first is Gene Amdahl, who in many respects fits the stereotype of the technical genius. He is indifferent to money except as an indicator

[1]Information on the Amdahl Corporation is drawn from "Gene Amdahl Takes Aim at IBM," *Fortune*, September 1977, pp. 106 ff.

Table 10.1. Type Complementarity

Intuitive Needs Sensing Type	Sensate Needs Intuitive Type	Feeling Type Needs Thinker	Thinker Needs Feeling Type
To bring up pertinent facts	To bring up new possibilities	To analyze, organize, to find logical inconsistencies and flaws	To persuade
To apply experience to problems	To provide ingenuity in dealing with problems	To weigh evidence	To forecast how people will feel
To read the fine print in contract			To arouse enthusiasm
To notice what needs attention now	To recognize signs of coming change	To fire people when necessary	To teach
			To sell
To have patience and persistence	To prepare for the future	To stand firm against opposition	To appreciate other types
	To have enthusiasm	To deduce conclusions from data	To bind people together in cooperative endeavor
To keep track of essential detail			
To face difficulties realistically	To recognize new, essential elements in a situation	To discover similarities and associations	To make a decision when the evidence is not conclusive
	To tackle difficulties with enthusiasm		To identify the unique and particular aspects of situation

Source: Adapted from Isabel Briggs Myers, *Introduction to Type*, 2nd ed. Copyright 1976 by Isabel Briggs Myers, p. 5.

of success, and is too involved with his thoughts to care about the everyday aspects of management. He appears to be an intuitive, as is evidenced by his creative insights expressed in his computer designs and by examples of what appears to be inferior sensation. For example, while pacing back and forth in the throes of engineering and design problems, he fell down the stairs of his house. His talent for computer design, as well as his often rigid adherence to principle, reflects strong auxiliary thinking.

In early 1974, Amdahl's newly formed enterprise almost collapsed. The main problem was the absence of management: key officers were simply unable to control and manage the rapidly growing business. Under pressure from outside financiers, Eugene R. White was appointed president of Amdahl Corporation in August 1974. White is described as a man whose practical talents are as impressive as Amdahl's conceptual abilities. He showed an enthusiasm for the administrative and managerial tasks that Amdahl loathed, and was responsible for a complete reorganization of the company, as well as a major reduction in staff. White, then, appears to be a sensate with auxiliary thinking. Not enough is known to arrive at any kind of firm conclusions, but it is likely that he is also an extrovert.

According to outside observers, the complementarity of Amdahl and White is extraordinarily effective. John Connolly, an Amdahl director who has known Gene Amdahl for decades, said that, "Gene White has added as much to Amdahl Corporation as Gene Amdahl has. They are exact opposites and the best pair of men I have ever seen teamed up."

The pairing is that of the intuitive having inferior or unconscious sensation matched with the sensate having inferior or unconscious intuition. The bridge connecting the two men is their auxiliary thinking.

Subjectively (that is, from the point of view of Gene Amdahl and Gene White), the relationship has been extremely difficult. Evidence of this is given by the fact that Amdahl and White have never been able to agree on a clear division of duties between them because of distrust and dissension between them and among the directors. As a result, they have ended up sharing similar responsibilities and do not mention a Chief Executive Officer in the corporate by-laws. However, it appears that the two men have acquired a genuine respect for each other that could lead to trust, and a conscious recognition of the value of dividing responsibilities along the lines of talent and interest.

PITFALLS OF PROMOTION

As I have already pointed out, people achieve their success in life largely on the basis of their superior or differentiated function. This one-sided development that served them so well can be the basis for subsequent failure if they are promoted to positions of responsibility requiring the use of functions that are unconscious or undeveloped in their previous experience. A good example would be the very successful salesperson or manufacturing manager whose success is based on highly differentiated sensation. On the basis of his or her success, this person is promoted to a general manager's position. The new position, that of general manager, requires not only that the individual sense what is actually happening in the actual, immediate situation, but also requires creative intuition to ensure that the organization not become stagnant and repetitive in its actions. It is not necessary that the individual in the general manager's job her- or himself possess powerful intuition but, at a minimum, she or he must be able to recognize intuition and value it enough to ensure that it is expressed in her or his organization.

The same pitfall occurs in reverse when the intuitive and creative marketing person is promoted to a general manager's position. In this new role, imagination and creativity are required, but in addition, he or she must also perceive and recognize what is actually happening on a day-to-day basis in the organization, to ensure that it does not begin to run out of control as he or she chases the endless new possibilities suggested by his or her own creative imagination. Again, it is not necessary that the chief executive possess highly differentiated sensation. However, it is absolutely necessary that he or she recognize and value this function in his or her collaborators, and ensures that these aspects of the organization's total performance are fully developed, and carefully reviewed and monitored.

CONFRONTING YOUR INFERIOR FUNCTION

One of the greatest values of the type theory is the insight it provides into our own weaknesses. Only if we have identified our inferior function can we consciously act to ensure that we draw on this function when necessary in life. To do this, we must consciously suppress the opposite or superior function. For example, the intuitive may find it necessary to consciously suppress intuition of possibilities in a situation in order to observe what is actually happening at the moment. Similarly, the thinker whose life is ordered by logical and impersonal thought must consciously suppress this function in order to focus on personal individual needs and concerns. In contrast, the feeler needs to suspend his or her tendency to particularize and individualize his or her response to a situation by backing off and addressing questions of logical consistency and sound structure.

As an example, consider a problem in organization design. The error of the thinker would be to ignore the individual and personal qualities, motivations, and capabilities, and attempt to design the "ideal" structure for an organization. The end product might be the best in theory, yet totally fail to respond to the human qualities of the people who are expected to work within this "ideal" structure. The error of the feeler would be to consider only the individual and personal capabilities, motivations, and concerns, and in the process ignore organization theory and logic. Clearly, a one-sided emphasis will lead to a less effective organization than one that combines both rigorous logic and adherence to valid theory, as well as recognition of the individual personal qualities of the people who will be working in the organization. In the 1960s, a period characterized by widespread enthusiasm for "going multinational," a number of companies adopted the sophisticated worldwide product division matrix design without taking into account that their people had inadequate experience for working in this structure. The result was disastrous. Managers with absolutely no understanding or experience outside the U.S. business environment attempted to manage businesses on a worldwide scale and quickly revealed their ignorance. On the other hand, if thinking is not present, the idea of the ideal design will not guide the development of an organization, and can lead to structures that are retained beyond their useful life in spite of their inefficiency and inappropriateness to a changing situation.

THE SUNAO SPIRIT

In Chapter 8, I referred to the *sunao* spirit, which Kono-suke Matsushita has identified as the most essential quality for management. The *sunao* spirit refers to an untrapped mind that sees things as they are, without special bias or preconceived ideas.[2] Obviously, the *sunao* spirit is an ideal. Every human being has biases and preconceived ideas, so Matsushita is talking about a goal to strive toward rather than a state that can be achieved. Having the *sunao* spirit is a commitment to developing the functions of perception—to working at opening up to seeing things as they are.

If you agree that the presence of the *sunao* spirit is desirable, the question is how do you acquire this spirit? According to Matsushita, acquiring the *sunao* spirit is like reaching the first *dan* in the game of *go*. (*Go* is the Japanese game that takes a lifetime to master. As checkers is to chess, so chess is to *go* in terms of complexity.) In the game of *go*, anyone can become a first *dan* player by playing about 10,000 times. Conversely, if one wishes to acquire the *sunao* spirit and spends each day searching for it for 10,000 days (or 30 years), he or she will achieve the first *dan*. At that level, according to Matsushita, you will avoid making any big mistakes because the *sunao* spirit will be at work in every aspect of your life.

The *sunao* spirit is the spirit of typological development. Reading this book is the first step in a lifetime of work to develop your capacity to see things as they are, and to make choices that not only reflect sound thinking, but also sound (i.e., conscious) feeling. If you feel

[2]Konosuke Matsushita, "The Untrapped Mind—The Philosophy of Management-20" *PHP*, November 1980, pp. 88–91.

that there is something in type theory for you, now is the time to begin your own 10,000 days of hard work to discover your own type, and to discover and develop your functions and attitudes. You must discover your type to be what you really are, and you must develop your functions to do what you need to do to be who you really are. When you discover your type, and when you develop your functions of perception and judgment, you will have the *sunao* spirit and will not make any big mistakes.

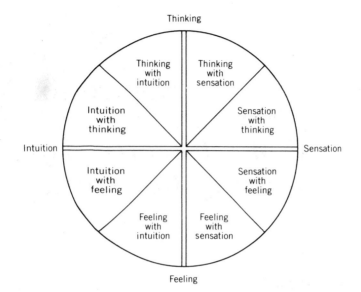

Thinking

Thinking
with
intuition

Thinking
with
sensation

Intuition
with
thinking

Sensation
with
thinking

Intuition

Sensation

Intuition
with
feeling

Sensation
with
feeling

Feeling
with
intuition

Feeling
with
sensation

Feeling

how you really feel and act, not how you would like to be or what you think others expect you to be.

Read each question carefully, *but do not take too much time with any question.* If the answers seem, on the first reading, equally valid, re-read and select the answer you feel is applicable to you most of the time, even if this is only a very slight preference. If after re-reading you still feel not even a slight preference, skip the question. After completing the questions, transfer your answers to the answer sheet.

Next, read the directions on the scoring instructions sheet and fill in the blanks and information requested.

PART ONE

Instructions: Parts one and two
Circle the letter of the answer or word that comes closest to telling how you *usually* feel or act, or the answer that best describes your natural or innate preference, *not* what you would like to be or how you act to meet the expectations of others.

Appendix

KTMI: Keegan Ty[
Measuring Instrume[

INSTRUCTIONS

There are no "right" or "wrong" answers to the qu[
tions on this indicator. Your answers will help you ide[
fy your preferred way of perceiving reality and of mak[
decisions or judgments. The indicator is not based o[
theory of a "best" or "better" approach to perception a[
judgment. It is not a measure of "intelligence" nor d[
it attempt to identify any form of maladjustment. [
other words, there is no way to "pass" or "fail" or to g[
"good" or "poor" score on the indication of your o[
preferences. So, relax and answer each question [
honestly as you can. Honesty for this purpose mea[

1. Compared to others, are you
   a. comfortable in group situations
   b. somewhat reserved until you know people well

2. Do you feel you are more
   a. a fact person
   b. an idea person

3. Which do you usually prefer? Conclusions based on
   a. reason
   b. personal preference

4. Most of the time, do you prefer
   a. contact and interaction
   b. peace and quiet

5. My greater strength is
   a. attention to detail
   b. the big picture

6. Which of the following statements better describes your response to business or family problems?
   a. I am a consistent and fair person
   b. I am sensitive to the feelings of others

7. When telling a friend about something that you were involved in, most of the time do you
   a. describe what happened
   b. tell how you experienced the event

8. As a person are you more
   a. practical and to the point
   b. idea oriented and speculative

9. Which is more important in a conflict?
   a. the principles involved
   b. specific circumstances

10. In making decisions or choices, which do you weigh more?
    a. objective facts
    b. your own subjective feelings, perceptions, and thoughts

11. Which impresses or strikes you more?
    a. a person's accomplishments
    b. a person's potential

12. Are you more
    a. a person of principle
    b. someone with strong preferences

13. When arguing, do you tend to
    a. stick to facts and adjust your position as new facts are introduced
    b. generalize and rule out conflicting views regardless of "facts"

14. Is keeping track of your financial affairs
    a. a cinch
    b. a challenge

15. Are you more
    a. logical
    b. emotional

16. Are you
    a. open about yourself to others
    b. somewhat reserved

17. Do you tend to
    a. finish projects before going on to something new
    b. tend to go on to something new before finishing existing projects

18. In working with others I tend to become impatient with

a. people who express ideas that are not thought out
b. people who put too much faith in their logic and analysis

19. When you meet someone new, do you open up
    a. fairly quickly
    b. only after spending some time together

20. Do you find yourself tempted to undertake new pursuits
    a. not too frequently
    b. quite often

21. Which do you find more interesting?
    a. social and political problems
    b. friends' problems

22. Compared to others, I am
    a. easy to get to know
    b. somewhat reserved

23. I am more aware of
    a. what is
    b. what might be

24. Admitting that both are important, would you prefer to work on
    a. social problems
    b. individual problems

25. In making judgments, which is more important to you?
    a. objective facts
    b. subjective facts

26. Which appeals more to you?
    a. known facts
    b. ideas and concepts

27. When making a tough decision, which is your better guide?
    a. your head
    b. your heart

PART TWO

28. a. outgoing
    b. reserved

29. a. down to earth
    b. imaginative

30. a. understand
    b. empathize

31. a. objective
    b. subjective

32. a. doing
    b. ideas

33. a. fairness
    b. sensitivity

34. a. outward
    b. inward

35. a. present
    b. emerging

36. a. theory
    b. instance

PART THREE

Instructions: For the following questions fill in the number 4, 3, 2, or 1 to indicate which alternative is most like you. Use the numbers in reverse order:

4 for the ending which is most like you

3 for that which is the next best description

2 for the next

1 for the description which is least like you

37. My strongest suit is my ability to
____ a. be practical and realistic
____ b. know and express my own feelings
____ c. use my imagination
____ d. logically analyze a problem

38. I enjoy most
____ a. being logical and consistent
____ b. coming up with new insights
____ c. being in touch with the immediate here and now
____ d. expressing my own views

39. If my living were assured I would prefer a job where I
____ a. could concentrate on exploring new possibilities
____ b. could work with others to help them achieve their potential
____ c. could concentrate on designing and implementing a plan
____ d. could troubleshoot and make things happen

40. At meetings I make my greatest contribution by
____ a. focusing on the facts

____ b. being in touch with my own feelings and those of others
____ c. focusing on the possibilities
____ d. helping others to see things logically

41. I am
____ a. a systematic and consistent person
____ b. a person who can see the possibilities in situations
____ c. a pragmatic realist
____ d. a person with a good sense of what others are feeling

42. My attention focuses primarily upon
____ a. future possibilities
____ b. the present and how it relates to my experience and memory
____ c. the flow of time from the past through the present and into the future
____ d. the immediate present situation and what to do about it

43. When confronted with a problem, I most enjoy
____ a. focusing on the specific facts of the situation

_____ b. recalling previous instances where I have encountered similar problems

_____ c. imagining the possibilities of dealing with the situation

_____ d. sorting out cause and effect

44. When under pressure I may

_____ a. become too attached to a plan or program and fail to recognize specific circumstances

_____ b. get carried away with ideas and possibilities and ignore practical realities

_____ c. get too involved in detail and lose sight of the broader picture

_____ d. become too attached to my own feelings and ignore logical inconsistencies

Instructions: Transfer answers from Parts One, Two, and Three to Answer Sheet.

ANSWER SHEET

PARTS ONE AND TWO

Instructions: Circle the letter corresponding to your answer to each question.

Row Totals

1. a   4. a   7. a   10. a   13. a   16. a   19. a   22. a   25. a   28. a   31. a   34. a   a. _____I
   b   b   b   b   b   b   b   b   b   b   b   b   b. _____II

2. a   5. a   8. a   11. a   14. a   17. a   20. a   23. a   26. a   29. a   32. a   35. a   a. _____III
   b   b   b   b   b   b   b   b   b   b   b   b. _____IV

3. a   6. a   9. a   12. a   15. a   18. a   21. a   24. a   27. a   30. a   33. a   36. a   a. _____V
   b   b   b   b   b   b   b   b   b   b   b   b. _____VI

PART THREE

Instructions: For questions 37-44 write the number 4 under the letter corresponding to the ending which is most like you, the number 3 for the ending which is the next best description, the number 2 for the next, and 1 for the ending which is least like you.

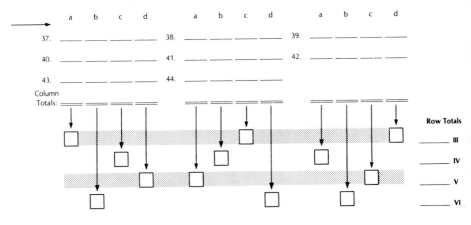

         a   b   c   d   a   b   c   d   a   b   c   d

37. ___ ___ ___ ___   38. ___ ___ ___ ___   39. ___ ___ ___ ___

40. ___ ___ ___ ___   41. ___ ___ ___ ___   42. ___ ___ ___ ___

43. ___ ___ ___ ___   44. ___ ___ ___ ___

Column
Totals:

Row Totals

_____ III

_____ IV

_____ V

_____ VI

Instructions: After transferring answers, follow scoring instructions on page 228 of question booklet.

SCORING INSTRUCTIONS

1. **Parts One and Two.** Count the number of a's and b's in each row on the Answer Sheet and enter the number in Row Total Column

2. **Part Three.** Add the numbers in each vertical column on the Answer Sheet and enter in the box indicated by the column arrow. Then add scores in the horizontal row of boxes and enter in Row Total Column.

3. Transfer Row Total Scores from answer sheet to the appropriate column below.

	Row Totals Parts One & Two			Row Totals Part Three	Total Score	Score Check
I E	_____ × 8			=	_____	
II I	_____ × 8			=	_____	96
III S	_____ × 4	=	_____ +	_____ =	_____	
IV N	_____ × 4	=	_____ +	_____ =	_____	
V T	_____ × 4	=	_____ +	_____ =	_____	176
VI F	_____ × 4	=	_____ +	_____ =	_____	

4. Perform the indicated multiplications and additions to find total score.

5. Check scores by comparing total scores with score check figure in last column.

6. Fill in boxes below:

  For E/I Box, fill in E if E > I. If I ≥ E, fill in I.
  For S/N Box, fill in S if S > N. If N ≥ S, fill in N.
  For T/F Box, fill in T if T > F. If F > T, fill in F. If T = F, and if you are male, fill in F; if you are female, fill in T.

7. Pre-indicator self-evaluation: Fill in boxes below with letter that corresponds to your type preference.

228

Appendix 2

Storywriting Assignment

If you are part of a group (class, department, club, etc.), one of the interesting ways of exploring your own type preferences is to complete the storywriting assignment. The first part of the assignment is to write a story describing the ideal organization. After writing your individual story, form groups of type-similar members[1] and come up with a group story. After the group stories are prepared, arrange for each group to make a presentation to the class on "The ideal organization." You will be amazed to see what a strong effect type preference has on preference for organizational structure and style. The individual and group assignments are described on the following pages in a format that can be used as a handout.

[1]The similarity can be in the combination of perception and judgment, that is, four groups consisting of thinking-intuitives and intuitive-thinkers; thinking-sensates and sensate-thinkers; feeling-intuitives and intuitive-feelers; and feeling-sensates and sensate-feelers.

Storywriting:
Individual Assignment

_____

_____

Write a short story that expresses your conception of an ideal organization. In your story, describe the characteristics and qualities of the heroes in your ideal organization.

The stories need not be of great length or form. You might, for example, make a straightforward description of the characteristics and qualities of the ideal organization, or you might alternatively describe what it would be like to spend a day, a week, a month, or a year in the ideal organization.

Storywriting:
Group Assignment

Organize yourselves in any manner. Discuss each individual story and come up with a single group story that best expresses your group's concept and description of the ideal organization. Summarize your group's ideal organization on a flip-chart for use in presenting your group's conclusion to the class. Select one or more members of your group to present your conception of the ideal organization to the class.

Index

decision-making ability,
64–65
self-knowledge of, 53
subordinates and, 200–203
unconscious feeling and, 32
Einstein, A., 142
Elliot, John, Jr., 130–131
Emotions, creativity and,
147–148
Empathy, subordinates and,
201
Eros, business and, 178–179
Eulogy writing, feeling
exercise, 167–168
Evans, P. A. L., 199
Expressive style, of
management, 45–46
Extroversion, 15–16, 18–19
characteristics of, 23–24
of master inventor, 59–61
Extroverted ego, 191
Extroverted/intuitive leader,
case example, 159–164
Extroverted sensation, 60
Extroverted style, of
organizations, 122–127
Extroverted type, 16–17,
23–25
outer-direction of, 160, 161
strengths of, 102

Fallows, J., 108
Falsification of type, 207–209
Family oriented organization,
IBM, 164–165
Feeling, 151–184
absence in communication,
77–78
awareness by speaker, 76
explanation of, 28–31

function of, 7–8
Japanese management,
173–176, 179
making of a leader, 180–181
unconscious feeling, case
example, 153–159
Feeling function:
development of, 165–166
feeling exercises, 166–173
Feeling style organizations,
119–120
Feeling type, 28–31
communication styles, 73
inferior function of, 39
listening ability, 67
management and, 68
strengths of, 102
time orientation, 88–89
Flavin, J., 159
Ford, Henry, 89–90
Forward Product Planning
Committee, 90–91
Frequency of types, 187–189
Freud, S., 39, 139
Friendships, using intuition
about, 133–134
Functions:
auxiliary and third function,
44–45
dynamic interaction, 58–59
inferior function, 38–42
interaction with attitude,
59–61
opposition of, 34–38
relationship to the
unconscious, 42–44
sensation and intuition,
25–28
thinking and feeling, 28–31
Future time, intuitive type
and, 96–97

JuNG

2 - DIMENSIONS

    1. ATTITUDE: INTROVERSION
                      EXTROVERSION

    2. APPROACH TO PROBLEMS

        a) INTUITION
        b) THINKING
        c) FEELING
        D) SENSING